UNDERWATER FLIES
FOR TROUT

UNDERWATER FLIES
FOR TROUT

TOM FULLER

DRAWINGS BY DARLENE CZAPLA DEWHURST

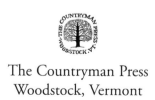

The Countryman Press
Woodstock, Vermont

To Pat,
whose counsel, support,
admonitions, intelligence,
and listening ear are surpassed only
by her love, tenderness, strength,
and independence as my partner,
best friend, and wife.

Library of Congress Cataloging-in-Publication Data
Fuller, Tom, 1948–
        Underwater flies for trout : a comprehensive guide to subsurface forage, flies, and tactics / Tom Fuller ; illustrations by Darlene Czapla Dewhurst.—1st pbk. Ed.
                p. cm.
        Originally published: Camden, Me. : Ragged Mountain Press, c1996.
        Includes bibliographical references (p.)

ISBN 0-88150-602-8
        1. Flies, Artificial. 2. Trout fishing. 3. Trout—Food. 4. Aquatic insects. I. Title.
SH451.F855 2003
799/1'757—dc21

2003048929

Interior design by Dan Kirchoff
Cover design by Eugenie S. Delaney
Cover photo by Brian O'Keefe
Black and white photographs by Pat and Tom Fuller
Color photographs by Tom Blomstrom
Illustrations by Darlene Czapla Dewhurst

Published by The Countryman Press, P.O. Box 748, Woodstock, Vermont 05091
Distributed by W.W. Norton & Company, 500 Fifth Avenue, New York, NY 10110
Printed in the United States of America
10 9 8 7 6 5 4 3 2 1

CONTENTS

Color plates of popular fly patterns
    appear between pages 86 and 87.

FOREWORD

I was glad when Tom asked me to write the foreword to his book—I'd get to read it before anyone else, and I'd end up catching more trout than I usually do by this time in the season.

Underwater Flies for Trout lays out in clear, succinct terms how trout behave and feed, then profiles various trout foods, useful imitations, and effective presentations. *Underwater Flies for Trout*, in a nutshell, affords a comprehensive approach to fishing trout flies beneath the surface of all waters, big and small, rushing and still.

Tom draws on a remarkable breadth of material, skillfully building on the work of the masters of the underwater fly, creating a unified whole from the disorderly world of subsurface imitations. Reading *Underwater Flies* reminded me of Hawkeye Pierce's line in *M.A.S.H.*: "I like reading the dictionary because it's got all the other books in it."

This book is accessible and useful to anglers of all levels. It retains the practical, problem-solving approach I find so useful. What do you do, for example, when you just can't seem to imitate the particular caddis pupa the fish are taking? Most of us dig out our "Old Reliable" and flail away across and downstream. After reading this book you'll be armed with a half-dozen strategies, each suited for a particular situation.

This is a no-nonsense guide to catching more trout. Plain and simple. You won't see

much of the author on stage; it is the material that remains front and center. The result is that you can open the book to any page and start becoming a better angler right away.

I've fished trout and landlocked salmon with Tom Fuller for more years than I want to remember, and you couldn't ask for a better companion astream. He always drives, never complains, and eats or drinks whatever you set down in front of him (I'm cook). He always has an extra set of hackle pliers or extra lantern mantles.

We've taken trips to the West Branch Ausable, Housatonic, Farmington, Battenkill, Lamoille, Androscoggin, and the grand landlock rivers of Maine. Had good fishing sometimes, bad fishing other times, and always a lot of fun.

I can't tell you how often he's taken trout from pools I'd given up on. And it's never due to some Olympian casting feat or secret fly. It almost always goes like this: I plow through the brush, flushing game as I go. Tom waves me through, then sits on a rock, smokes his pipe, watches me froth up the water. I give up and collapse on the bank, panting like a played-out bird dog. Tom walks over to my spot, knots on a fly, roll-casts 20 feet in the current with his 7½-foot rod—and hooks the fish I didn't realize was there. Later at night, when everybody else at camp is trying to put a few inches on the trout they caught that day, you'll see Tom jotting down the day's action in his diary.

In a way, reading this book reminds me of the time we've spent on the stream. He sees so much about what's going on under the water, is quick to share his information — but slow to take credit for figuring it out.

So rest assured that Tom's own substantial experience trout fishing is the basis for this book. A born and bred Yankee, with home rivers in New England, he has also fished extensively the great rivers of the West. What you'll find here is the finest blend of research and experience, a book that is both insightful and practical, one that will put you on to more fish from day one.

As I said, it's done that much for me already.

WILL RYAN
Northampton, Massachusetts

INTRODUCTION

Underwater flies predate any other type of furred and feathered imitation intended to catch trout. They were around long before Dame Juliana's famous treatise, and they may well have been the first artificial lures, dating back to ancient Egypt. Being first on the scene doesn't necessarily make them the best at catching more and bigger trout—it just happens to work out that way.

Throughout their long history, underwater flies have, like many enduring ideas, waxed and waned in popularity. Exclusively used in Europe to catch wild trout at one time, they were vilified as unsporting and unfair by the turn of the 20th century. Movements arose to outlaw underwater flies, and river keepers throughout Great Britain banned any angler audacious enough even to suggest their use. It was unfair to the trout and dangerous to the health of the fishery, or so fly fishers of the era thought.

It is that dangerous effectiveness that lights up our modern perception of underwater flies. They fell out of favor because they were too effective. What chance did the trout have if they were to be barraged with imitations that easily and often fooled them into thinking they were taking natural food items? And why, in the late 20th century and in the midst of our current passion for exact and detailed imitation, hasn't the underwater fly become the premier artifi-

cial of each and every fly fisherman?

The answer, of course, involves the vagaries of human preference, individual perceptions of the aesthetics of fly-fishing, and the angler's need to catch trout within self-imposed parameters. The most practical anglers, those whose goal is to fool as many of the biggest fish as possible, will invariably end up using underwater flies most of the time.

Indeed, in the current controversy about whether fly-fishing has become something of a snob's game, the real culprit is the angler who espouses only one method, usually dry-fly fishing, over all others. Most anglers who use artificial flies exclusively know through their own experience that their artificials work better than almost all other methods of fooling trout. At times dry flies are unbeatable, especially when the trout are looking for their meals on the surface. But during the vast majority of the time that an angler can be on the stream, the fish will be feeding underwater, and that's where the angler should be floating his fly.

Underwater flies have varied functions. Nymphs imitate the immature forms of mayflies, caddis flies, and stoneflies. Streamers and bucktails represent an entirely different food source. Emergers fill the niche somewhere in between immature and mature insects. And traditional wet flies appeal to a fish's aggression, curiosity, or appetite for a specific food item.

Of these fly types, nymphs appeal most to us because their function is the most understandable. They imitate a food item we know is available to the trout and is regularly consumed by the trout, and we attempt to convince the trout to inhale our nymph as if it were a natural.

Much the same can be said about emergers, which are gaining in popularity. Because trout prey on insects when they are most vulnerable, namely, as they attach to the meniscus and emerge from their nymphal shucks, this class of underwater flies becomes very important, if only, like dry flies, at specific times.

Imitation is also the reason that many of our streamers and bucktails are so effective at attracting big trout and salmon. Originally, these longer, leaner flies simply gave an accurate imitation of feed fish and their movements. As experiments have broadened with streamers, however, and as the flies have developed beyond strict imitation into more gaudy patterns, their success can be more accurately ascribed to a different motive in the trout.

What exactly that motive is, we aren't sure. And because we can't accurately describe what these flies are doing or why the fish are interested in them and aggressive toward them, we tend cautiously away from them. Yet it was these same gaudy, colorful flies that started man casting toward trout in the first place. Wet flies, those enigmas of design and function that worked so well they were banned on many English streams, remain curiosities. We don't always know why they work. They don't always imitate prey naturally, so they must appeal to the trout for other reasons. Are the fish aggressive toward gaudy wets because they are out of place? Is there some instinct in trout that inherently suspects anything out of the ordinary in their home water? Or do trout have some innate curiosity that anglers have yet to define and exploit?

These traditional wet flies confound our sense of logic, but they work, much as the "attractor" dries work on the surface. And we should certainly appreciate the mystery of their effectiveness, much the same as Atlantic salmon anglers or Pacific steelheaders appreciate the effectiveness of their gaudy imitations. Why does the Royal Coachman wet fly work so well? For many of the same reasons that the Royal Coachman dry fly works so well.

In the pages that follow, we will examine as best we can what underwater flies are intended to imitate, how they do so, how an angler must present the fly to achieve this imitation, which fly patterns are the most effective, and why, in a few cases, all this logic and observation are irrelevant. Each chapter offers a unified core of facts about its particular subject, in the hope that every fly fisherman can find some new bit of information somewhere in the book.

Our fascination with the imitation of naturally occurring food items is well founded on the ongoing observations and experimentations of generations of curious and successful anglers. Their passion for imitative underwater flies is their pleasure and ours.

The anglers of both current and bygone eras will also guide our discussion of the attractor flies, but their logic, as we may gleefully discover, is either wrong or intentionally lacking. To our infinite enjoyment, we don't know yet why fish strike these flies. But we're happy they do, and we appreciate the anglers who have so diligently experimented, largely out of blind faith, with new ideas about fly design and use.

The work that anglers generally and writers specifically have done on under water-fly fishing falls far behind that done on surface-feeding fish and floating flies. And probably it always will, because it's much easier to observe activity on top of the water than in it. It's also a fact that modern fly fishermen parallel society in general in their need for relatively quick gratification. Actually *seeing* a fish rise to a fly, whether or not the fish is hooked and landed, is often enough for an angler to claim success.

It takes considerably longer for an angler to become wholly involved in all aspects of aquatic life and his interplay with it, and only those who are in for the duration have the patience or develop the curiosity to study underwater life, flies, and fishing.

DECISIONS, DECISIONS! THE BASICS OF CHOOSING A FLY

Which fly do I tie on? It is the basic question for any fly fisher. This book and countless others have been written to answer it.

An angler stepping into a stream in Oregon, Michigan, or Vermont in April, June, or October must first have put some imitation onto the end of his tippet. If he is familiar with his stream at the time of year he is on it, the decision may not have been difficult. Many streams have followings of devoted anglers who have documented among themselves, and often for publication, just which insects emerge at what times of year. Local information is invaluable where it is available.

But an angler new to an area or to a particular stream, or on a familiar stream at an unfamiliar time of year, confronts the tough question of which fly to start with. Should it be a mayfly imitation or a caddis? Would streamers or big flies be appropriate? What about attractor wets? What happens when a stream at a particular time of year has a unique hatch?

The vagaries and subtleties inherent in choosing the appropriate fly form the core of our fascination with fly-fishing, but fundamental logic can be applied to the selection process.

Observation of the stream and what's

happening around it is the key to determining which forage the trout are focusing on. If we can actually see fish sipping mayfly duns or caddis adults from the surface, and can catch and closely observe an insect, then we know not only what the fish are feeding on at the moment, but also what they are probably feeding on under the surface before and after the hatch.

Without a hatch, we need to sample what's available in the flow of the stream, or to be more diligent in finding stream-bank clues as to which insects have been available, or to use our past experience on similar water types to decide which fly to fish.

The following rough outline will help us on our way. As we gain particular experience on certain streams and general experience on many water types, the selection process should, but doesn't always, become easier.

1. If the insect you are inspecting is on the surface and has upright wings and three (two less commonly) slender tails, it is a mayfly. See Chapters 2, 5, and 7.

2. If the subsurface insect you've collected in your sampling net has the same two or three slender tails, external gill filaments attached to the abdomen, wing pads on the back of the thorax, and single claws on its feet, it is a mayfly nymph. See Chapters 2, 5, and 7.

3. If the insect you're inspecting is mothlike, has pup-tent-like wings, has no tails, and flies quickly off the surface of the water, it is a caddis fly. See Chapters 3 and 6.

4. If the subsurface insect you've collected is grub- or wormlike, if you're seeing many small stick or pebble cases on the bottom, or if your sampling reveals nearly fully formed adults in chitin pouches, none with tails, suspect caddis flies. See Chapters 3 and 6.

5. If the mature insect you're finding on the surface, or especially in streamside vegetation or on rocks or logs, holds its wings flat against its back, has two stout,

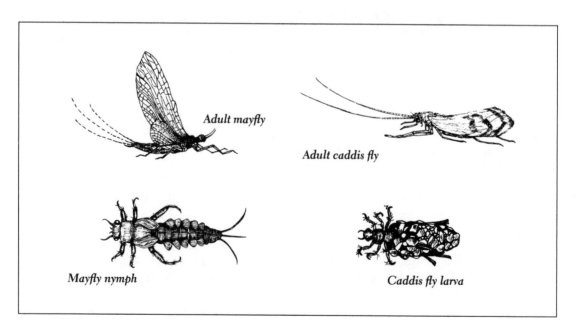

Adult mayfly

Adult caddis fly

Mayfly nymph

Caddis fly larva

Adult stonefly

Streamer—Gray Ghost

Stonefly nymph

Soft swimmer—matuka

usually short tails, and two claws on its feet, it is a stonefly. See Chapter 4.

6. If the subsurface insect you've collected lives in highly oxygenated water, has two tails, and has two claws on its feet, it is a stonefly nymph. See Chapter 4.

7. If you know or suspect that large trout are available, if you've seen schools of forage fish, and/or if you're targeting the largest fish available, use streamers or soft swimmers. See Chapters 8 and 9.

8. If you can't classify your forage as any of the above, see Chapter 11.

9. Everyone should read Chapter 10, on wet flies. They are the foundation of fly-fishing, imitate many of the insects and other forage found in trout waters, and offer excellent choices for searching the water or for fishing when you've got no clue as to available forage.

1

UNDERSTANDING UNDERWATER TROUT FOOD

The goal of any study we do about the feeding preferences of trout is to fool the trout into taking our imitations. To improve on our imitations and tactics we need to understand the base upon which successful angling has been built. By studying, first of all, the three major orders of insects and by understanding the interaction between the trout and these food items, we can begin to form a more focused strategy for taking advantage not only of the trout's preferences but also of their alternate food sources. And this may help us to catch more and bigger trout in a greater variety of situations.

All fly fishermen can identify with the excitement of watching a decent trout sipping surface insects. There's a pulse-quickening joy in approaching a new pool, unsure of what, if anything, you might find and, as you stare into the water, in having a good trout show on the surface. In addition to bringing a smile to your face, it confirms several solid bits of information.

The first is that you do indeed have trout available in the water you've chosen to investigate. This is no small tidbit. In southern New England, for instance, where I do most of my fishing, many streams are either very heavily fished, with an astounding trout mortality rate, or they are marginal water and support only hatchery trout in the spring.

I enjoy getting out anytime I can, and I appreciate the pleasures of simply escaping office, job, or family responsibilities for a few quiet moments on the stream. I am also fully aware, however, that the reason I carry a fly rod and struggle down the stream bank dressed in bulky waders and a bulging fishing vest overstocked with flies and fly boxes is to cast to and catch trout.

For me, the trip isn't complete if I haven't had a trout on the line, or at least seen one. I am, at best, a poor barren-water angler. That first rise of a trout on new water ends my obsessive search for good trout water. Even on familiar water, a single quick rise bolsters my confidence that I am exercising my efforts over trout.

Major Orders of Insects

The second bit of information a rising trout conveys is that insects are available in the water. In most cases, these insects are indigenous to the stream. They have spent the great majority of their lives in the water and have become exceptionally vulnerable to the trout during that hazardous time when they transform from water- to air-breathing creatures. Later in the year, rising trout may indicate that terrestrial insects have fallen

The ring of a rise on trout waters usually ensures that trout are present and feeding on insects, and that they can be taken with good imitations.

Trout showing on the surface may indicate that the fish are taking underwater insects. In this illustration, from left to right, the trout could be taking mayfly emergers in the film, following caddis pupae, or following caddis adults returning to and breaking through the surface.

into the water and are floating along, but during the spring and much of the summer, the insects trout are rising to are often stream-dwelling creatures.

Finally, once you know that trout are present and actively feeding on stream-born insects, you can safely assume that at some point the trout can best be caught with underwater flies that imitate some form of those insects. When the trout are concentrating on surface insects, it would be ludicrous to suggest that subsurface artificials are more productive. But as more and more anglers and writers are recognizing, rising trout do not always indicate surface feeding.

Many times, a trout that shows itself on the surface is actually feeding just below the surface. The insects are often unsuccessful in the struggle to complete their life cycle, and they can be stuck on the bottom of the meniscus, that mysterious boundary between water and air. The trout find these hapless creatures particularly appealing. Sometimes the insects are at their most vulnerable just before emerging onto the surface film, their struggle to escape their nymphal or pupal shuck giving the trout their best opportunity to feed. Or the trout may be most attracted to these important food sources as they ascend from their normal streambed dwellings to the surface.

We can be fairly certain that while a surface-feeding trout verifies these several bits of information, the same trout does the great majority of its feeding below the surface. For all the excitement we feel in spotting and casting to rising or surface-dimpling trout, they actively feed below the surface much more often. Some experts, in fact, state that trout take in as much as 90 percent of their nutrition below the surface. Thus we can be fairly sure that accurately imitated underwater insects will greatly improve our angling success and our catch rates.

Since the vast majority of trout feeding is subsurface, envisioning which flies to use and how to present them requires an understanding of what the trout are feeding on and where. If you can identify the food items and learn a bit of their natural history, it becomes relatively easy to imitate them, both in the fly you tie on the end of your leader and in the way you present it to the fish.

While feed fish and crustaceans are important components of a trout's diet and will be discussed later in this chapter, insects are by far a trout's primary underwater food. And three kinds of underwater insects account for most of the food available to and consumed by trout. Among other factors, water quality, temperature, oxygen content, current speed, and bottom makeup determine where these insects are found, but often all three cohabit the same river or stream and even the same stretch of water.

Their names are perhaps familiar to anyone who has taken up a fly rod. They are mayflies, caddis flies, and stoneflies—in their order of preeminence on the surface, not underwater.

Mayflies dominate surface angling for a number of reasons, not least of which are their fragile beauty and the focused attention of several generations of highly skilled anglers, fly-tyers, and writers. Caddis flies are more mysterious, if no less important to the trout, both under the water and in the air. They possess a vitality that defies quick study or imitation. The most prominent family of underwater insects, however, is the stonefly.

STONEFLIES

Stonefly nymphs are seductive to both trout and anglers for two good reasons. In the first place, most of them are big. It must be difficult for any trout, particularly a large one, to let such an attractive meal go by, no matter how well fed the fish or how attuned to some other more abundant food. Stonefly

With no visible surface activity, the author took this 17-inch brown trout on Connecticut's Housatonic River with a bottom-bouncing Hare's Ear Nymph.

nymphs sometimes reach 2 inches in length, and even the smaller species are invariably larger than the other insects with which they share the streambed.

In addition, where they populate a stream, stoneflies are in residence at nearly full-grown size all the time. This may not seem particularly earthshaking at first, but it is important because they are the only prominent aquatic insect that can make this claim. Mayflies and caddis flies have only a one-year life cycle in most cases, and therefore are important only as they reach their final development and grow large enough for the trout to notice.

Stoneflies are always available because

Stoneflies crawl about on the bottom of fast, well-oxygenated water and usually hatch out of the water on rocks, trees, or shrubs.

they take three to four years to mature in the rubble and fast water of the streambed. When the oldest nymphs mature and migrate toward the shore to hatch out, one-, two-, and three-year-olds remain in the stream. And by age three, their size is impressive and attracts the trout's attention.

In their pursuit of longevity, stonefly nymphs stay well hidden in the rocks and rubble of their preferred fast-water habitats. Wherever highly oxygenated fast, rough water occurs, the biggest stoneflies can be found clinging to the bottom. These large flies are usually tan, dark brown, or black, though some do take on a distinctly yellow tint.

If we are to cover all the varieties of stoneflies, we can generalize that they all have the same basic look: two tails, six legs, two wing coverts, and a fairly uniform diameter from front to back. While there are many, many species, and their size ranges from ⅜ inch to 2½ inches, the bigger species

are well enough dispersed for us to concentrate on them.

Because they are big and are known to crawl about looking for other insects to prey upon or for a good dinner of greens, these insects occasionally become dislodged by the hard currents they prefer. They can't swim a lick and float along the bottom until they bump into something on which they can get a foothold. The trout don't need to see a number of them pass by before becoming interested but will pick them up whenever they can. Even just a single insect drifting by will draw a trout's attention.

Although trout will key on stoneflies at times, specifically as they make their mass migration to shore (most of them hatch out of water), most often they are an incidental meal. Trout will pick them up even if they haven't seen another nymph go by for a week.

The stonefly's life cycle has one fewer phase than the mayfly's and two fewer than the caddis's (see illustration, page 45). From eggs that some adults drop over the water, but that are more often *dapped* (placed during flight) through the surface film, nymphs

Typical stonefly water is rough-and-tumble, pure, and well oxygenated.

are born one to three weeks later. Depending on the species, the nymphs will live on the bottom from one to four years, progressing through many life stages, called *instars*, between molts. These nymphs can be either vegetarian, like the giant salmon fly *(Pteronarcys californica)*, or carnivorous, like the golden stones *(Calineuria californica)*.

When the time arrives for them to emerge as adults, the mature nymphs migrate across the bottom of the stream and crawl out onto rocks, logs, or the shore. Once on dry land, the fully formed adults step out of their nymphal shucks and mate, generally after dark.

The smaller stones may survive in this adult form for only a day or two, but the larger stoneflies may live as long as two to three weeks. The egg-laying flights containing concentrations of the larger stoneflies can be quite impressive, with masses of flies dapping the water. But more often, these flights are sporadic and, especially in the East, occur after dark.

MAYFLIES

Mayflies rank next to stoneflies in importance as underwater food for trout. They are abundant in many types of water, can range from small morsels of food to substantial mouthfuls, and are available wherever trout

Mayfly nymphs are important in all sections of the stream: dwelling on the streambed, rising through the water column, and attaching to the meniscus.

water flows. They include one more stage in their development than stoneflies, progressing from egg to nymph to air-breathing dun (subimago) to spinner (imago). (See the life-cycle diagram on page 19.)

Because most mayflies live a one-year cycle (some have shorter cycles and more than one generation a year, and some take up to two years to develop), the variety of different types provides an interesting and broad array of options for trout to choose from and anglers to study. Literally hundreds of species exist throughout North America, and any one might be particularly important on a particular stream.

A number of mayflies, however, are widespread across the continent and have become well known. Green Drakes (*Ephemera guttulata*), Brown Drakes (*Ephemera simulans*), Hendricksons (*Ephemerella subvaria*), and the like have developed followings where

they occur on good trout streams. Many fly fishermen gladly schedule their lives around the regular, predictable hatches of these insects.

By successfully imitating them in their nymphal form, subsurface anglers can produce good catches for as long as two to three weeks before the nymphs actually begin to emerge. As a particular species of mayfly approaches its traditional hatching time, the nymphs are at their largest and most active, and the trout home in on them.

Mayfly nymphs can be classified into four basic groups, namely, clingers, crawlers, swimmers, and burrowers. All of them have six legs, two or three tails, gills for breathing, a thorax, and an abdomen. They all spend the vast majority of their time in and around the rock, rubble, sand, and detritus of streambeds and lake bottoms. They feed on microscopic plankton, vegetation, and the occasional insect they can catch. Mayflies spend at least 95 percent of their life cycle in this form underwater.

While mayfly nymphs vary greatly in length, from only a fraction of an inch to more than 1½ inches, their colors do not cover a wide spectrum. As you might expect, most take on the colors of their immediate surroundings—earth tones such as tan, brown, gray, dark olive, and black.

Of the four basic types of mayfly nymph, three are found quite logically in the water type that matches their physical characteristics: Clingers have overly developed legs and are designed for holding tight onto rocks and rubble in fast water. Burrowers prefer a soft bottom of silt and leaves so they can burrow relatively undisturbed. Swimmers need light flows of riffle water and occasional still water so they can get from one place to another without being swept away. But crawler nymphs, as their name implies, move by crawling around, and they can do that almost anywhere.

The type of water you are fishing is important in how you present a mayfly nymph. While the pattern and size of a fly are also important, correct choices there may prove fruitless if your presentation fails to match the water. Again, logic dictates.

Because crawlers and clingers depend on being attached to something for their motility, a rock or a log for example, they are rarely available to trout unless they become dislodged. When that happens, they are helpless and simply float along with the current until they can reattach themselves to another solid object. Free-drifting an imitation close to the bottom without any drag or motion from the fly line is the best tactic.

As the water slows down in riffles, pools, and backwaters, the swimmers and burrowers become more prevalent, and here a certain amount of movement in the imitation will help. The crawlers that sometimes frequent these water types can help themselves by swimming too, so motion will make even their imitations more attractive to the trout. In pure still water, like lakes and ponds, an angler gives all the motion to the mayfly nymphs.

Simply stated, mayfly nymphs are bot-

In the pools below rapids and riffles, mayfly swimmers find their best habitat.

tom dwellers, and their imitations must be fished there much of the time, but the action an angler gives to his nymph imitation is directly related to the water type in which he is fishing. Fast water requires a dead drift. Still water requires nymph motion from the angler. But more on angling patterns and tactics later.

Caddis Flies

Caddis flies are proving to be the most reluctant of the water-born insects to give up their secrets. Several recent innovative and extensive studies have thrown much light on caddis flies and their place in stream entomology, but the sheer number of their species, along with their reluctance to spend much time as a surface food item for trout, maintains their reputation as the least understood subsurface item of all. Yet they might be the most important to the trout.

Caddis flies are the only one of the three important insect types to enjoy a full complement of developmental steps (see illustration, page 31). From eggs that are sometimes dropped onto the surface or more often literally carried to the bottom by the mature adult, tiny larvae hatch in a few days to a few weeks. Caddis flies spend the majority of their life cycle in this larval form, and most of the larvae construct some sort of pebble, twig, or shredded-leaf home. A few others are free-living forms that construct intricate underwater nets to capture their food, and a few more are completely free-living.

As they reach maturity, within one year, they seal up their housing or create spun cases and pupate. In these cases they metamorphose into mature adults. When it is time to hatch, the fully formed adult, inside the pupal case, floats to the surface with the aid of a gas bubble, or in some cases swims to the meniscus, and emerges.

The underwater larvae of caddis flies are not as important to the fish as stonefly or mayfly nymphs for one basic reason: with their elaborate housing, they are relatively fortified. Though these larvae are unable to change neighborhoods and may occasionally be fed upon by trout rooting around on

Caddis flies live as free-roamers, often rappelling on silk; as net makers; or as case builders.

The downstream drift of a caddis-imitating wet fly produced this hookup for the author.

the bottom, the fish are more inclined toward easier meals that don't come with a load of pebbles or sticks attached.

The caddis pupae attract the most attention from the trout and, consequently, the angler. It is when the pupae mature and ascend to the surface that they become the trout's favored food. In this stage they add the important element of availability to the equation of what trout eat and when they feed.

Caddis pupal forms are not very well suited to underwater movement. Indeed, most of them are slowly propelled upward by a gas bubble in the pupal case, and even the swimming emergers are not terribly quick at thrusting themselves to the surface. It is during this drifting rise from bottom to surface that they are most vulnerable to trout predation, offering an angler his best opportunity to take advantage of trout feeding on a caddis life form.

When these pupae do reach the surface film, they attach to it and emerge from their shuck and fly away. Since they are fully formed and ready to fly, trout feeding on them do so with hard quick rises, for they know their meal will swiftly escape if they aren't decisive.

Trout also feed on the adult underwater forms as they dive and swim down through the water to attach their eggs to the bottom. During both their descent and their return to the surface, they are vulnerable and at their most visible, with their fully formed wings reflecting light and pinpointing their position.

Trout also take surface egg-laying caddis flies. But these flies don't sit and wait for trouble. They skitter across the surface, touching down occasionally to drop eggs and quickly moving on. Trout after these adults must also be quick and often completely clear the water as they slash out after the caddis.

Two more major characteristics of caddis flies increase their importance to trout and to anglers. First, they hatch in fewer numbers and over a longer period of time than mayflies do. Generally, their emergence covers many hours during each of several days. This extended emergence may be due to their decreased vulnerability on the surface and in the air shortly after they hatch. They don't need to stand around waiting for their wings to dry. They are strong fliers immediately upon hitting the air because they are fully formed during pupation.

Second, they are long-lived adult insects. The process of breeding and egg laying may take several weeks, during which they will make many trips back to the water and expose themselves to trout predation again and again. They are available as feed, albeit not in great numbers, for a much longer time than mayflies.

This important factor adds unique opportunities for using underwater caddis imitations. Many modern anglers are partial to mayflies, but accurate and well-presented caddis imitations can often outfish mayfly imitations, especially when the trout are not focused on a mayfly hatch an hour or two away.

Our best trout streams are a fertile soup holding a diversity of life that interacts in ways we, as anglers, may not have yet imagined. Indeed, even within the three families of insects considered so far in this chapter, much remains to be studied and learned. But we do know that these families offer most of the opportunities for trout to feed. They may not necessarily offer most of the food, however.

Feed Fish

Indeed, most scientists are sure that once a trout reaches about 10 inches in length, it needs to take in larger food items to grow bigger and heavier. In most cases this means that the trout will attack and consume prey outside the insect world — logically, other fish.

Depending on the mix of feed fish available in a given body of water, the trout might concentrate on a particular type of smaller fish, as they do in New England when they feast on smelts, or they might be pure opportunists, taking nearly any living item they can fit into their mouths, such as sculpins, chubs, crayfish (which can be extremely important), or other smaller trout or salmonids. This suggests that we devise the appropriate imitations. Specifically, streamers and bucktails were invented hundreds of years ago to take advantage of these larger prey and attract bigger fish.

But again, knowing which flies are effective in which waters requires a thorough understanding of what's available. Trout must at least be familiar with a particular item of larger prey, even if they don't need to see a lot of them on a particular day before they will attack. They will not attack if the imitation is entirely foreign to them.

Yet, with this said, streamers and bucktails that are only impressionistic imitations of available feed fish often work best. And gaudy attractor streamers, such as the crimson Cardinelle or the yellow and red Mickey Finn, are at times unparalleled. The one cohesive fact about streamers and bucktails is that they must act like feed fish. Their movement in the water and their presentation must imitate the natural feed fish that the trout are accustomed to. And often these actions of the artificial are direct results of

To maintain their growth after maturity, larger trout must supplement their diet with larger prey than insects.

the construction of the fly. How the angler presents them is important but secondary to proper materials, proper fly silhouette, and careful assembly.

Be aware that even the larger fish that attack other fish do not stop taking insects. Often, as they become accustomed to a particular food item, say, a mayfly nymph, on a particular day, they won't be swayed from that food item by the appearance of, say, a chub. They'll probably ignore it altogether because their nutritional needs at the moment are being satisfied by the nymphs.

But by and large, when the energy value of a large morsel is greater than the energy loss required to capture it, a big trout will be sorely tempted. While smaller artificial nymphs and wet flies might be carefully inspected before a strike, a streamer ghosting across the head of a pool can often trigger an immediate attack.

Feed fish are a primary food source for larger trout, and fertile waters hold many of the bigger prey, including these crayfish and sculpins.

Other Food

Although these major families of insects and the feed fish form the foundation of nutrition in the majority of trout waters, other organisms can be important to anglers, too. Many limestone streams and fertile still waters are literally full of scuds and sowbugs. Minute midges can overwhelm a stream with their sheer numbers. Craneflies, alder flies, and dobsonflies can't be ignored. Damselflies and dragonflies can rival stoneflies in size and importance. And leeches, eels, fish eggs, even drowned terrestrials— all will find themselves preferred food in certain waters at certain times.

The habits of observation we form over the years, and the methods and imitations we find most comfortable and most productive, help us form a procedure that we follow almost by rote. This procedure will serve us well in nearly all situations if it incorporates the principle of an open mind and the capacity to explore and question what we find.

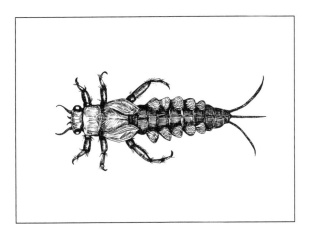

2
MAYFLY NYMPHS

No angler worth his wading skills ignores mayflies. They are the most obvious of surface food items and certainly the most important to dry-fly anglers.

Compared with the time anglers spend studying and imitating the duns of mayflies, however, the effort given to the subsurface forms of mayflies is negligible. This is indeed surprising considering that mayflies spend fully 95 percent of their lives underwater. It seems even more inequitable when we realize that the time nymphs spend on the stream bottom and rising to the surface is almost always longer than the stay of hatched duns on the meniscus. The pre-

hatch underwater activity includes an extensive period of restless preparation, when the nymphs shift from their long feed-and-grow stage to their inevitable rush to the surface. They begin to get restless, to move about, and in their watery world this makes them vulnerable to trout.

Their vulnerability becomes acute when they actually begin their ascent. They are out of the protective cover of the rocks and rubble of the streambed. Their swimming skills are, at best, rudimentary—certainly no match for trout. And they often must make more than one attempt to reach the surface film, rising through the water and dropping back, only to rise again.

Most anglers are oblivious to the underwater acts of the drama of prey and predator, of the rush to air by mayflies, and the rush to eat them by trout. It is, rather, the final act, when the duns must spend those often disastrous few seconds drying their wings on the surface, that fascinates us most because we can see it.

This fine brook trout came from New Hampshire's Perry Stream and took a deep-drifted Hendrickson Nymph some two hours before the hatch actually occurred.

Observation, Study, and Written Records

The basic problem with studying and imitating underwater mayflies, especially when their prehatch activity excites trout to feed, is that we can't see them. With duns, the problems of identification and imitation can be easily solved by plucking one of the helpless creatures from the surface and matching it. And in no way is this process to be

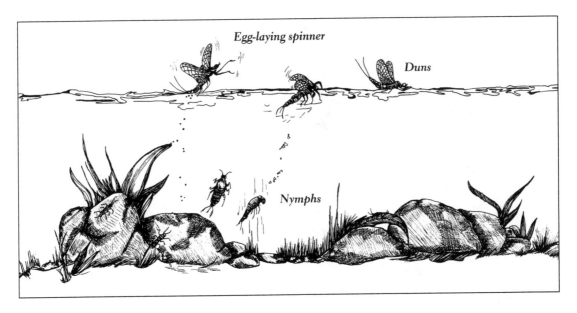

Egg-laying spinner

Duns

Nymphs

The mayfly life cycle progresses from egg to nymph to dun (subimago) to spinner (imago).

minimized, as dry-fly angling's great popularity is centered on it.

But by expanding this process, by using our firsthand experience and observation in collecting and examining mayfly duns and nymphs, we can home in on what's available to the trout before and during the hatch and, to a degree, after it. I carry a little aquarium net in my vest to do just that, and I use it to catch drifting duns, to pluck the occasional emerger from just below the surface, or to grub around in the shallows. I've also got a more substantial homemade streambed sampler (just some vinyl screen mesh stretched between two dowels), and I use it either when I'm stumped about what's happening on a stream or when my more analytical evil twin demands additional detail.

Checking the natural nymphs we've collected in any one of several excellent and exhaustive published studies will give us

precise identifications. The combination of curiosity, logic, and resources can help us pinpoint which insect we are seeing or can expect to see, and we can then accurately imitate it.

First of all, our own experience and observation will serve us very well. Knowing that certain water temperatures at certain times of the season have produced a specific hatch on a specific water in the past, we can fully expect that same hatch again. Mayflies are quite timely and are, happily for us, destined to adhere to an annual cycle. If the sulphur hatch occurred on the stream across the street during the last week in May last year, then we can certainly expect it again this year. And we can reinforce our expectations before the hatch is due by looking under a few rocks for the nymphs that will become sulphur duns.

Even on streams where we don't have personal experience, much of the information we have gained will apply. If the water temperature and the amount of daylight available on a particular spring day produced Hendricksons on our home water,

Even in pure, clear mountain streams an amazing array of organic and inorganic matter drifts by; anglers must learn which food items the trout have focused on.

Publications

With a solid reference work like *Hatches II*, or the Orvis handbook *Trout Stream Insects*, or Art Flick's timeless *Streamside Guide*, we can supplement what we are learning about our own particular stream and the food it produces for trout. We can verify an initial identification of a nymph or mayfly, or we can apply what we know of where and when a nymph turned up to find its name and the standard patterns and sizes of the artificials. Again, blending observation and experience with resources and logic, we can adhere to or alter, as needed, the patterns that imitate the insects found on particular streams.

then those same conditions may well produce Hendricksons on other streams.

To make use of the information we've so painstakingly gained over the years, we must keep a record of it. How we do that is a matter of personal preference. I'd love to have an encyclopedic memory, but I don't, so I write it down. My reference work is a simple journal. Somewhere in each entry, I've noted the important information about water temperature, weather, time of year, and so forth. But my journals are more narration than data, and I enjoy going back over them to rekindle memories. More analytic folks might prefer daily logs. But make some sort of record.

Specifically, what we are looking for and trying to imitate are the size, shape, and color of the naturals available to the trout when we are on the stream.

Scientists have established that trout do not automatically ingest anything that simply looks like a meal, especially when the energy equation is not heavily weighted on the nutrition side. Simply stated, the energy derived from a food item must be equal to or greater than the energy a trout expends to capture it. And thorough studies have shown that trout do not automatically switch to new food items.

The trout's experience with the energy equation underlies the importance of our knowing which hatches are impending or in progress. Uncertain whether a new food item is nutritious, or dangerous for that matter, a fish will usually ignore what might appear a tempting morsel.

Hatches

In what we think of as pure water, an astounding array of bits and pieces of organic and inorganic matter floats down through a trout's feeding area. Experimenting with every piece of material that floats by would absolutely ruin a trout's energy equation, so he sticks with what he knows. But this simple "eat what you know" tactic is complicated by the fact that much of a trout's food is available only in short segments of the year.

Studies have also shown that as particular food items become more plentiful and regular—specifically, as mayfly hatching times approach—trout will experiment with them; when the experiments prove the new items to be nutritious, the trout will focus on them.

The value of this strategy is more apparent when we examine the mayfly's life cycle. The eggs that most mayflies deposit into the water are both tiny and, once attached to the bottom of the stream, immobile. The tiny nymphs that hatch out of the eggs are insignificant to a trout both because they are usually hidden and because they are too small to meet the requirements of its energy equation.

Only as they reach their last instars and become active, and thus available, do they gain importance as trout food. As the trout see more and more of them floating by, they initially experiment with them and then gradually begin to focus on them.

Of equal importance to subsurface anglers, the trout maintain their focus as the yearly hatch tapers off. A hatch does not often begin at full steam and end at its peak. Most hatches, in fact, begin sparsely and build to a climax. Well after the climax has passed, a few laggard nymphs still struggle to the surface. This tapering is fairly universal.

Because the trout have become attuned to taking the nymphs associated with a hatch, they will continue to gobble up even very occasional individuals as the hatch passes and stops altogether. For up to two to three weeks after a hatch has stopped, trout will still take the nymphs associated with it.

All this study of which mayfly nymphs are doing what and when they're doing it answers two basic questions for the angler: which fly pattern should he tie onto his leader and how should he present it to the trout.

Mayfly Nymph Imitations

The problem with discussing mayfly imitation in any general way is the huge variety of water types and insects an angler is likely to encounter. Modern economics and transportation make it easy and inexpensive to travel throughout North America. An angler can drift a fly through the picturesque freestone streams of New England one day and ply the limestone slicks of Pennsylvania the

The Gold-ribbed Hare's Ear artificial imitates a broad variety of nymphs. The Isonychia *nymph is imitated by the Zug Bug, the Brooks' Ida May, and other artificials.*

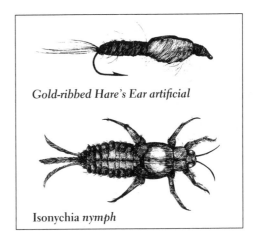

Gold-ribbed Hare's Ear artificial

Isonychia *nymph*

next. He can move on to the fertile variety of streams in the Upper Midwest and finish his odyssey on the brawling waters of the Rockies. And he can do it all in the space of a short vacation.

Much of the fascination of fly-fishing centers on this variety of experience. New waters always offer new challenges, and as a fly fisherman becomes enamored of a particular type of water or even a single watershed or stream, he can take the basics of imitation and refine them to very specific heights. But first he needs some basic knowledge and a core collection of artificial flies. With subsurface mayflies, that means nymphs.

CORE PATTERNS

The essence of this core collection is versatility. An angler wants to keep observation and study at a minimum and productive fish-

The Gold-ribbed Hare's Ear Nymph is the centerpiece of any collection of mayfly nymph imitations.

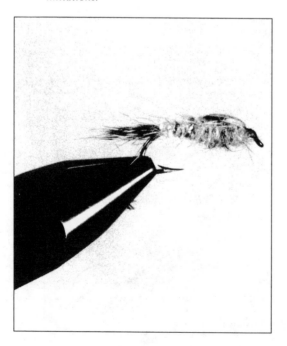

ing time at a maximum. As he gains experience, he can expand or refine his core collection to suit his habits, but always he needs to concentrate on size, shape, and color. Here's a basic selection of mayfly nymphs, mine, that might be a good starting point.

GOLD-RIBBED HARE'S EAR.

If I were limited to a single mayfly nymph, it would be the Gold-ribbed Hare's Ear (see Plate 1). The subtle color of its material, literally the fur from the ears and face of a European hare, and the variety of textures of this same material make it a universal choice. It imitates quite specifically several very important mayfly nymphs, like the Quill Gordon, March Brown, and Green Drake, but its utility lies in its bugginess.

Because so many mayfly nymphs either resemble the Hare's Ear or are specifically imitated by it, trout are attuned to the general profile and color of the artificial throughout the season. The variety the angler needs to add is in the size of the fly and the area of the stream in which it is fished.

The Hare's Ear should be carried in sizes ranging from big #8s down to about size 14. Again because of the nature of the material, flies tied much smaller than this become somewhat dysfunctional, looking more like clumps of fur than good imitations.

Most hare's masks have some color variation too, from tan to dark brown, and these colors can be emphasized as an angler becomes more focused on the nymph he is trying to imitate.

The question of where and how to fish the Hare's Ear relates to whether the fly is weighted. Because trout usually find their meals along the streambed, that's where most nymphs should be fished. Even when an angler manipulates the nymph, as discussed later in this chapter, he is usually going to try to move the nymph from the bottom of the stream up through the water column, so he needs to start near the bottom.

With some of the smaller pattern sizes, the profile of the artificial would be hurt with the addition of wire wraps for weighting to the underbody. Not so with the Hare's Ear. It's a pretty big fly anyway, so attaching the lead or tin wire to the hook itself when the fly is tied is better than taking the fly to the bottom with split shot on the leader.

Nymphs with built-in weight are preferable to weighted leaders, simply because they will drift more naturally and provide a more direct connection between the rod tip and the fly. They don't have the interruption of the piece of split shot between them.

When emerging or stillborn mayflies are being imitated and the pattern needs to float in or just under the surface, unweighted nymphs, particularly Hare's Ear Nymphs, are deadly. (Emergers will be discussed in Chapter 5.)

HENDRICKSON. My second core nymph is the Hendrickson (see Plate 1). Although the pattern, roughly a brownish burgundy body with black wing cases, does indeed imitate the maturing nymph of that spectacular and famous hatch, the Hendrickson in but a few sizes also imitates many other species, like the black quill (size 12), the mahogany dun (size 16), and the sulphur dun (size 16). Three sizes, 12, 14, and 16, can cover a broad range of natural nymphs.

The differences here are that the body and thorax are tied with fine, spun dubbing fur and the color of the fly is much darker than any Hare's Ear. When wet, the burgundy brown fur and black wing cases give the Hendrickson a very dark, earthy look.

Again, the nymph should be weighted to put it down near the bottom, but a few flies should be tied unweighted, even on fine-wire hooks, to be fished on or near the surface during the hatch.

OTHER CORE PATTERNS (see Plate 1). My third core nymph is somewhat generic. It's smaller, tied in sizes 18 through 24, and has an olive brown body and black wing cases. In the smaller sizes it is very functional for the late spring and summer hatches. However, it produces well for much of the season because the nymphs it imitates are in front of the fish for a very long stretch and the pattern will draw strikes almost all the time.

The fourth nymph is an imitation of the later-season mayflies, like the Cahills, which have a lighter, tan tint and lighter wing cases. Tie the pattern in sizes 12 and 14.

And finally a small Black Nymph imitates those prolific tricos. They're a late-season mayfly, but can provide plenty of action from the height of summer on into the first frosts of autumn. Sizes 18 to 24 make them tough to create and often tough to tie onto a 7X tippet, but they are worth the effort.

With this core of nymphs, an angler can approach most angling situations, but as he becomes more and more familiar with what's happening in the stream, he can fine-tune the patterns and add others if he wishes.

In my experience, imitation can certainly be improved through closer observation when that observation translates into specific pattern changes in size, color, and shape. But also, my experience tells me that my tinkering usually produces variations of the artificials in my core group. Perhaps a darker shade of hare's ear fur, or a lighter yellow dubbing, or a size larger hook would provide a closer resemblance to the natural in a particular stream.

Mayfly Nymph Presentation

Effective presentation is as important in fishing mayfly nymphs as choosing the right pattern. Too often, an angler tries to change his luck by changing his fly, instead of changing how it acts in front of the fish (which is not always as easy as it sounds). And then the fly being presented incorrectly is also the wrong fly.

As explained earlier, mayfly nymphs can be divided into four basic groups: clingers, crawlers, swimmers, and burrowers. Only the crawlers can be found in several different types of water. The other three match up well with particular water types. The types of water in which he is fishing dictates how an angler will present his nymphs most of

Effective presentation of a free-drifting nymph is a practiced art, as illustrated here by Will Ryan on the upper Connecticut River.

the time. In slow water, where most swimmers and the burrowers live, he must give his nymphs some action. In fast water, where clingers are found, he should free-drift his nymphs. And in riffle or pocket water, the domain of crawlers and clingers, his presentation should be a combination.

DOWN IN THE WATER COLUMN

Swimmers and burrowers are slow- and slackwater dwellers, though some swimmers prefer riffle and pocket water. They are all good swimmers, but the effect of water movement on them will help an angler determine just how much action he should give his fly.

In slack water, with muddy or sandy bottoms, the burrowers must supply all their motion. As their name indicates, these big flies, like the Green and Brown Drakes, spend much of their time down in the sand and silt. But as they grow, they go through many instars, up to 30 a year, and every time they molt they leave their burrows. It's an active time for them, as they swim about trying to shed their old husks before returning to their homes. This activity dictates that you let an artificial fly settle to the bottom and then twitch it in nervous, active runs. Expect a strike as the fly rises, but let it settle back down to the bottom between active movements.

For the swimmers, which dart about in a number of slack-, slow-, and riffle-water habitats, a more vigorous action is needed. These flies swim in spurts, sometimes resting and drifting between spurts, but always regaining their movement. Their spurts can take them up from the bottom or across it, but they move. Straight-across or across-and-downstream casts that can be well controlled and manipulated are best.

Clingers love fast water, and they don't swim well, if at all. When they become dis-

In slow waters, swimming nymphs prevail, and the angler must give some motion to his imitation, as the author shows here on the First Branch of Vermont's White River.

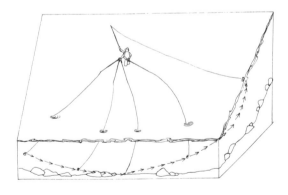

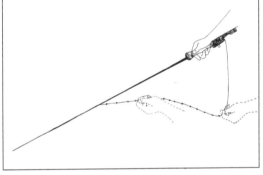

When an angler needs to give his mayfly nymph motion, he does so with short strips of line to imitate the quick darting motion of the naturals.

Crawling nymphs require some imagination in their presentation. A good way to start would be to free-drift the nymph along the streambed until the end of the drift and then swim it up to the surface, as shown here.

lodged, they simply free-drift, usually near the bottom. Weighted nymphs drifted through their preferred heavy water flows or in the heads of pools at the ends of these flows work best. Try to maintain a fairly straight line to these free-drifted imitations so you can detect strikes and set the hook;

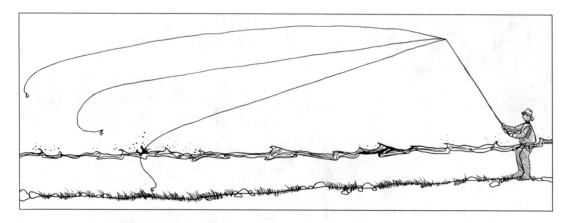

The upstream tuck cast helps present a free-drifting clinger-type nymph. By overpowering the cast, the angler makes the fly swing under the fly line before it settles onto the water and drifts near the bottom.

but don't swim the imitations, drift them.

The crawlers are the most problematic when it comes to presentation. They can and do swim, and they inhabit a variety of water types, so the best approach is to vary what you are doing in a particular stretch of stream. Free-drift a nymph down through pocket water, but if it swirls into an eddy behind a rock or log, twitch it, give it some life. Alter your presentation. Swim the nymph along the bottom through slot water, or let it tumble into feeding holds. Be creative and imaginative.

It is important to note here that these methods of presentation apply to the weighted nymphs an angler should be carrying and fishing on the bottom.

UP IN THE WATER COLUMN

For unweighted nymphs, used when a hatch is impending or under way, presentations are a bit different. These nymphs are generally fished on or just below the surface. They represent mayflies in the process of trying to hatch. The flies are still active. They are, after all, trying to get to the surface to split their shucks and emerge. An angler needs to be aware of this activity and should try to make his imitation do what these hatching nymphs are doing. Since he hasn't got the room—the amount of water—that he has when fishing the bottom, he needs a lighter hand. The action he gives to the fly should be subtler, making the fly move toward the surface a bit and then retreat. Often, just free-drifting a nymph or emerger pattern is best, but again, observation will be the main determinant.

Observation is just as important in determining whether to fish weighted, bottom-hugging nymphs or unweighted nymphs and emergers. When you're prospecting a stream and that flash of a fish near the bottom indicates that he's feeding there, it is neither logical nor productive to be offering artificials anywhere else. The opposite is also true. If the fish are bulging and feeding within a foot of the surface, bottom-hugging presentations are much less effective than emergers. But within the area where fish are feeding, top or bottom, manipulating the nymph according to what the natural can and can't do is important.

Tackle

Tackle recommendations are touchy areas for some folks. They're fond of vast collections of rods and reels, and seem to believe that rod length and line weight must be matched to a dizzying variety of water types and sizes, and types of fly-fishing. I've got neither the inclination nor the cash surplus to own such vast assortments of tackle, and for most of my angling one rod and two lines are plenty.

The rod is a six-weight generic graphite, 9 feet long. One line is a floater, the other a sink tip. If the depth at which I want to fish is no greater than my leader length, I'll use the floating line. If it is greater, I'll switch over to the sink-tip line. So much for rods and lines.

In my opinion, an angler should be much more concerned with what's happening out at the end of his fly line, and that means tapered leaders, tippet, and fly. For deep work with weighted nymphs a 7½-foot leader with a short, 1½- to 2-foot, tippet is sufficient if the leader and tippet are long enough to get the nymph to the bottom. If the water is slow and deep, extend the length of the leader and tippet as needed. The "rule of fours" is as good as any when determining tippet size: divide the fly size by four to get the tippet size you should be using. For a size 12 fly, use a 3X tippet, for example.

For fishing up in the top foot of water in the stream, I often use the same 7½-foot leader but with a 3-foot tippet, or I might go to a 9- or 12-foot leader with 3 feet of tippet, depending on how smooth the surface is. Trout looking up into the light are more sensitive to surface disturbances, and smooth surfaces are like crystal-clear windows.

One other piece of gear is very help-ful—a small bottle of paste floatant. By carefully applying it to the leader and tippet to a length just short of the depth at which you want your unweighted nymph to float, you can keep the leader and tippet on the surface and the fly at the right depth.

In a short chapter like this, it is impossible to cover all the species, actions, active periods, and natural history of the hundreds of families of mayflies. As mentioned, however, many excellent and exhaustive studies on both the entomology of mayflies and the methods and means of collecting and classifying them are available to anyone wanting

Will Ryan took this trout on Connecticut's Farmington River by drifting a Hendrickson Nymph just under the surface at the beginning of the hatch.

to further his studies into specific hatches and the natural lives of these insects. I would specifically recommend Caucci and Nastasi's *Hatches II*.

But the angler who first and foremost wants to catch more and larger trout will find that the patterns and methods covered here substantially increase his productive hours on a stream. By building up his own experience, honing his powers of observation, and then applying good imitations in a lifelike manner, he can take nearly full advantage of the trout's fascination with mayfly nymphs.

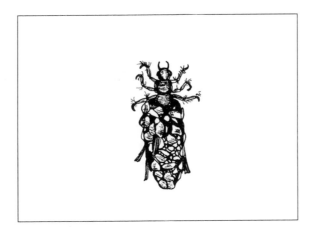

3
CADDIS FLY
LARVAE AND PUPAE

Caddis flies remain a mystery to anglers for a number of reasons. Chief among them is the short amount of time these flies spend on the water surface, either as newly hatched adults or as returning, egg-laying females. Unlike mayflies, caddis, because of the extra phase of their life, pupation, rise off the water quickly when they emerge. Because they live longer in their adult stage than mayflies, they don't return to the water in intense egg-laying swarms. And they don't simply mate, swarm over the water, and die as mayflies do when they create interesting spinner falls. In short, because caddis flies spend so much time out of an angler's sight, they are largely out of his mind.

In addition, there is a daunting variety of caddis flies. They comprise more than 1,200 species in North America alone and 7,000 species worldwide. There are black caddis and white caddis and any number of colors in between; there are brilliant green and orange individuals, as well as earthy brown, tan, and olive species. They can be tiny, as small as ½ inch, or huge, with some western species imitated on a 1/0 hook. Unless you're an entomologist tucked away in the biology building of the local university, how can you hope to sort out the complexities of caddis flies?

It is certainly an intimidating task, yet

more and more anglers are discovering that caddis flies may well be at least as important as mayflies in a trout's diet, and may indeed be more frequently consumed. Studying them will help anglers catch more and larger trout more consistently.

Luckily, dedicated fly fishermen and angling writers have been giving increasing attention to caddis flies. Foremost among them are Gary LaFontaine, whose 1981 book *Caddisflies* offers in-depth information on the biology and distribution of many of the most important caddis flies in North America. Preceding LaFontaine's book was Larry Solomon and Eric Leiser's *The Caddis and the Angler* in 1977, and even Schwiebert dedicated part of his classic *Nymphs* (1973) to caddis fly pupae and larvae.

What all of these authors, and more and more anglers, point to when they talk about caddis flies is that the best way to imitate them to catch trout is with underwater flies. From Chapter 1 we have seen that the life cycle of caddis flies is complete, including egg, larval, pupal, and adult stages. In all but the egg stage, caddis flies supply forage to hungry trout. We have also seen that because of this complete cycle, the emerging adults are fully formed and fly from the water surface fairly quickly, especially when compared with mayfly duns.

That leaves the underwater stages of development as the best time to imitate caddis flies. It also helps to know that it is on these underwater stages that trout feed most voraciously. In their larval and pupal stages, caddis flies are a prime source of nutrition for trout. Later, in Chapter 6, we'll investigate the emerging adult that attaches to the bottom of the meniscus, and the returning, egg-laying female adult, which very often carries her eggs to the stream bottom. But in this chapter, the focus is on the immature forms of caddis flies.

Of the two forms, caddis larvae have the

A Fur Caddis Pupa took this brown trout on Massachusetts' Deerfield River when only an occasional adult dapped the surface.

distinct advantage of being available much of the time. In this stage they actively feed on algae, detritus, small organisms, and other animals, and they put on all their bulk and weight. Later, during the pupal and adult stages, few, if any, nutrients are ingested. This means that certain species of the larvae move about, both to find prime positions from which to feed and to find new sources of food. And even those species that don't actually move are often exposed to trout predation because of their feeding and case-building activities.

There are three forms of caddis larvae: case builders, net builders, and free-living forms. Case builders are those insects most of us have seen on the streambed that have constructed small homes of sand, gravel, sticks, or vegetation. Net builders are similar to underwater spiders, using their nets both to catch prey and to filter food items from the water flow. Free-living forms are gener-

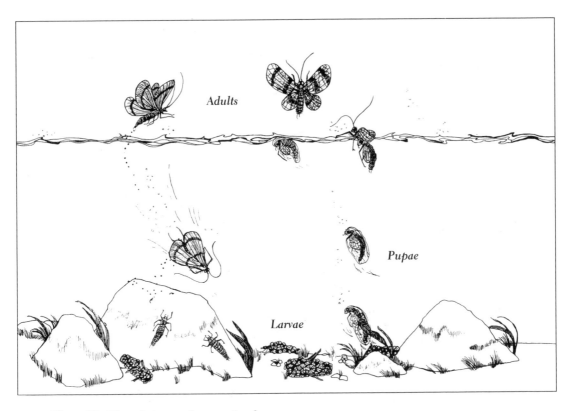

Adults

Pupae

Larvae

The caddis life cycle is complete, moving from egg to larva to pupa to adult.

ally predators, moving about and seeking other organisms on which to feed.

Trout will feed on any of them but would much rather have their meals delivered by the natural flow of the stream than rut about in the rubble of the streambed. So they prefer the net builders and the free-living larvae. And of these, trout are more likely to encounter the free-livers because these roaming insects often use the stream current to get about and often are simply washed downstream. But free-living caddis larvae also use the silk that all larvae can generate to rappel or anchor themselves to something solid (see illustration, page 32), and we can try to imitate those movements with our flies.

Trout do not, however, ignore the net builders or the cased larvae altogether. As hungry opportunists, they have no aversion to picking off these bits of food when they're available. I've even watched good trout grubbing, literally churning up the streambed, then swimming downstream of the cloud of debris and picking off the food items they've disrupted. Often these food items are caddis larvae. And trout will swallow cased larvae, sometimes turning on their sides to scrape the cases off against rocks, at other times pouncing on larvae emerging from their cases to expand their homes or build new ones.

When the larvae have completed growing, which usually entails five instars or molts, the case builders seal off their cases, and the free-living and net-building forms build cases in which to pupate. Pupation is that mysterious metamorphosis that miraculously chan-

Case builders are the best-known caddis larvae, but free-living larvae are fairly widespread and often move from spot to spot by rappelling downstream on silk they produce.

ges bugs to beauties, worms to butterflies, and caddis larvae to winged adults.

For our purposes, it is not the actual process that interests us but the last step of the pupal transformation from water-breathing creature to air-breather. When the pupal pod, which is a pouch of chitin containing the adult, emerges from the pupal case and rises to the meniscus, trout pay attention. In most cases, the adult generates tiny gas bubbles in its pouch after it emerges from its case on the streambed, and it then floats and swims to the surface. When it reaches the meniscus, the pouch effectively helps break the surface tension and splits; the adult steps out, fully formed, and flies away.

These two forms, larvae and pupae, are what we are trying to imitate with the flies we tie and in the way we present them to the trout.

Caddis Fly Larvae and Pupae Imitations

A good core of caddis larva imitations does not include many patterns; six or seven different types cover nearly all needs. In fact, some anglers might tell you that two or three patterns are plenty, as long as you vary the color and the hook size. LaFontaine ties just two types of larva imitations, the cased and the uncased, and has proven very successful. But for many of us, blind faith in just one type of fly is difficult; therefore, I've included my seven core patterns.

As we'll see when discussing presentation tactics, many tyers insist on adding weight—either lead wire or the new nontoxic tin wire to the structure of the fly, or a brass or tungsten bead to the fly's front. Note that lead in any form in fishing, as split shot or built into flies, will soon be illegal, so make the transition to nontoxic materials now. Anything that helps maintain the correct position of the fly (which with caddis larvae is on the streambed) is fine as long as it doesn't alter the fly's basic shape, color, or natural float.

CORE PATTERNS

The first imitation in my core of caddis larva patterns is the Breadcrust (see Plate 2). The standard pattern calls for a burnt orange floss or wool body, a brown quill or mono-cord rib, and a soft grizzly hackle collar. It's effective and easy to tie, can be tied in a variety of sizes, and, although purists might cringe, is often tied in a variety of colors, particularly brown, olive, bright green, and gray. It has endured because it works. Sizes 8 to 16 should suffice.

Solomon and Leiser, in *The Caddis and the Angler*, described the Latex Caddis Larva, made by cutting strips from cream-colored latex, winding them over a weighted hook shank, and then coloring the latex with a marking pen. The effect was very real and produced well. Since then, inventive fly-tying merchants have developed materials that do the job more easily, and may even have improved on the illusion created. The materials currently available are Larva Lace, Midge Larva Lace, and Flexi-Floss, and all make excellent larva bodies. They're already colored too, in a range that meets most of the needs for larva imitations. Just wrap the flexible material for a tapered body, stretching it where the taper is narrowest and letting it sit thicker as you approach the front of the hook. The head itself is tied with fairly coarse black or dark brown dubbing fur or with peacock or ostrich herl. Again, sizes 8 to 16 should cover most situations.

Solomon and Leiser also described the Caddis Gilled Larva (see Plate 2). They used green floss for the body and palmered a piece of peacock or ostrich herl up along the body to imitate those larvae with gills

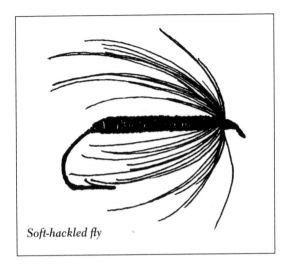

Soft-hackled fly

along their bodies. Gold wire was counter-wound over the herl to protect it, and the fly was finished with a herl head. It is an effective pattern, and experiments with a broader range of body colors have proved useful. Tie the fly in sizes 12 to 20.

Gary LaFontaine's Free-roaming Olive Larva pattern (see Plate 2) is simple to tie and versatile. With a few color variations, it can cover most caddis larva situations. The fly consists of a dubbed body ribbed with a brown hackle quill, a larger and darker dubbed thorax, and some grouse fibers under the throat of the hook to imitate legs. The dubbing mixes natural and synthetic materials. Color variations include olive, olive brown, yellow, pale green, and pink. Sizes range from 12 to 20.

CASED CADDIS LARVA PATTERNS. For cased caddis larvae, there have been some very inventive concoctions, although many are difficult to tie and fish. Some of them include the actual material the larvae use for their cases, and present complex structural problems by trying to imitate the square twig or sand cases. They could take hours to tie and seconds to lose. But a couple of patterns are both easy to tie and effective on the stream.

The first is the Brassie (see Plate 2). It imitates a cased caddis very well, and although many anglers think that its name means that it should be tied only with brass wire, gold, copper, or red wire can be used effectively. Tie it by simply wrapping the wire up the hook shank and adding a dubbed black head. It's tied in sizes from 12 to 20, but the smaller hooks are used most often.

The other cased caddis imitation that adds the dimension of versatility is the Strawman, as modified by LaFontaine. A grouse body feather, instead of deer hair, is wrapped along the back two-thirds of the hook shank and clipped to imitate the case. It can be clipped round or square, clipped smooth or left ragged. The front of the hook is wrapped with fur dubbing to imitate the larva peeking out of the case, and a few soft-hackle fibers under the throat of the hook imitate legs. Add weight to this pattern only on the rear half of the hook so that the fly will float with the larva's head up.

LaFontaine's greatest contribution in *Caddisflies* was a pattern of his invention that accurately imitates the chitin pouch surrounding the fully formed adult caddis when it emerges from its pupal case. All previous fly patterns had simply imitated the rising adult form with its stubby-looking wings. By introducing Antron yarn, a triangular nylon fiber that tends to trap tiny air bubbles, and tying it to specifically imitate the pupal pouch, LaFontaine filled a void. His Sparkle Pupa (see Plate 2) remains the best imitation and greatest fish getter when caddis flies are hatching.

The Sparkle Pupa may seem difficult to tie, but a little practice makes it relatively easy. Two unwound bunches of Antron yarn are tied in at the bend, one on top and one on the bottom, and are loosely brought forward over a dubbed body. Some hackle barbs, grouse or woodduck, are tied at the front of the pouch on the sides of the hook to imitate legs, and a head of herl or fur is formed. The pattern is tied on standard dry-fly hooks, from size 12 to 18. Some imitations are weighted so they can be fished deep. Core color combinations are brown head and yellow body and pouch, brown and bright green, tan and ginger, and gray and gray.

Caddis Fly Larvae and Pupae Presentation

If there were just two generalizations an angler remembered about using caddis fly larvae and pupae imitations, they would be Fish them deep and Fish them any time. And if there were a third, it would be that all generalizations have exceptions.

CADDIS LARVA PRESENTATION

For the larva patterns we've just listed, the "deep and any time" maxims are pretty accurate. If you have no reason to be fishing some other type of fly, fish a caddis larva or pupa imitation. In other words, if there aren't any fish obviously rising and feeding either on the surface or just under it, and if there isn't an impending hatch you've been waiting for all year (like the Green Drake), then fishing a caddis larva or pupa makes good sense. And if you're fishing a caddis larva, fish it on the bottom.

The idea in fishing these larva imitations, as it is with most mayfly nymphs, is to free-drift the fly down and through a trout's feeding lane. The larvae are helpless in the

Pat Fuller's success with Sparkle Pupa imitations is illustrated by this typical Deerfield River, Massachusetts, rainbow.

water flow, but when they are washed away, they leave a bottom structure and they stay near the bottom until they can reattach themselves. To successfully imitate the natural then, there must be no line drag and the fly must stay deep.

The subtleties of deep-drifting any free-floating fly quickly become apparent to an observant angler. There are three basic pitfalls to be recognized and avoided. The first is that the fly isn't floating deep enough; the second, that it's too deep and is constantly hanging up; the third is that it doesn't stay at the feeding depth long enough. Too often the solution to one of these problems creates one of the others. Not floating deep

enough? Add a hunk of split shot and get hung up on the bottom.

The art of properly fishing deep, free-floating imitations, in this case a caddis larva, is a matter of fine-tuning the length of the cast and the parts of the terminal tackle to match the conditions (see illustration, page 36). I wish there were one rig, say a 9-foot leader with a 3-foot 4X tippet section, with two pieces of microshot for a size 14 Breadcrust, that would work in all circumstances. There isn't. So experiment. But consider these suggestions when you do.

WEIGHTED FLIES. Unless you have reason to use a free-drifting underwater fly just below the surface, as you might with a Sparkle Caddis Pupa imitation and a few others, build some weight right into the fly. In most instances, the thorax section of the fly is at least a little larger than the abdomen, so put a few wraps of thin lead or tin wire there. A good rule of thumb is to use a wire with the same diameter as the hook. In many cases, such as shallow flowing water or slow-flowing water like limestone creeks, the built-in weight of the fly is enough to take it to the bottom.

The depth of the water and the speed of the current affect how long it will take your fly to get to the bottom. In a heavy flow within a deep chute of water, your fly might well be all the way through your target area before it gets deep enough. Your first option is to cast farther upstream, to lengthen the amount of time the fly has to sink. Always remember that it is much better to fish without added weight on the leader so that you maintain direct contact with the fly.

To effectively free-drift artificials along the bottom, it is often necessary to fine-tune terminal tackle, specifically leader and tippet lengths, as shown here.

If your fly isn't making it to the feeding level, add small bits of nontoxic microshot or some of the new moldable nontoxic weight. At first you'll have to guess how much to use, but with a little experience you'll make faster and more accurate estimates. And because you're using small bits of weight, you can add some or take some away easily. In each new run or type of water you fish, you'll want to be sure your fly is drifting at the level where it will be seen by the trout, so don't be bashful about tinkering with the weight. (A few regions of the country do not allow added weight on leaders, so check the local regulations.)

Only in the largest, deepest, fastest flows of water is it necessary to go to a sink-tip or full-sinking line, and even then it might be better just to use a longer leader and more weight. (Still-water situations are different, and that's where sink-tip or full-sinking lines are best.)

Also remember that maintaining direct contact with your fly means keeping your line as straight as possible. By keeping your rod tip low and pointed at the spot where your fly line enters the water, you can mend your line with gentle, quick flips of the rod as the line bellies. Inevitably there are varying tongues of current between you and

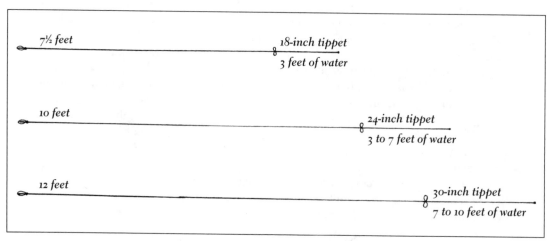

7½ feet   *18-inch tippet*
3 feet of water

10 feet   *24-inch tippet*
3 to 7 feet of water

12 feet   *30-inch tippet*
7 to 10 feet of water

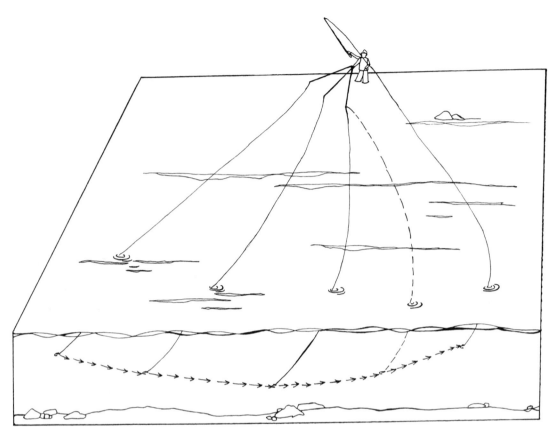

After free-drifting the artificial down and across stream, let it swim to the surface through the current, imitating a rising pupa.

your fly, so to keep the fly floating drag free and the line straight, mend the line. As your fly floats down toward you, you can raise the tip of the rod and strip in whatever line is necessary to maintain that good connection between you and the fly. And as it passes you, you can lower the rod tip and even play out some of the regained line.

CADDIS PUPA PRESENTATION

Use the straight-upstream or up-and-across-stream tactic for pupae imitations. Adjust cast length and line weight if needed, but

you can be a little more aggressive about keeping in touch with the fly. Your line can be a bit tighter on the water. The pupae are, after all, just drifting there, filling their chitin pouches with gas bubbles and anxious to start the ascent to the surface, so a little drag on your part doesn't hurt. It may even foster the illusion you're trying to create.

In fact, many good anglers add a bit of motion to a pupal imitation with short, 2-inch strips of line to imitate the natural as it tries to get moving upward. And there is a very famous tactic, invented and perfected by the legendary Jim Leisenring, that can be deadly if you know exactly where a fish is holding and feeding. It's known as *the Leisenring lift*, and it starts the ascent of the artificial just in front of the target fish. It is, by Leisenring's own account, a specialized tactic for particular situations, but it will often bring about quick, tough strikes.

With caddis pupae imitations you have another option, too. Remember that during a mayfly hatch, the duns must dry their wings as they float along on the surface, but with a caddis hatch not only can the adults fly away quickly, their hatching time is spread out over a much longer period. If there are few flies on the water but there is plenty of evidence of rising fish, then a pupal imitation floated just under the surface can be exceptionally productive because the pupae are mobile and the trout will station themselves higher in the water column when caddis pupae are rising and emerging. (At the height of the hatch, when you are seeing quite a number of adults, emergers fished right in the surface film may be more effective. This is discussed in the next chapter.)

By drifting a Sparkle Pupa Emerger just under the surface, the author took this early-season rainbow in Massachusetts' Millers River.

Perhaps the most common mistake anglers make when free-drifting larvae or pupae imitations, or mayfly or stonefly nymphs for that matter, is not fishing out the entire cast. They're so attuned to the idea of maintaining a free drift that as soon as there is any hint of drag at the end of the float, they immediately pick up their line and cast back upstream. Don't do that. Let the fly line tighten and move the fly up and across the current below you. Many times this bit of motion will trigger a strike, and with pupa imitations it mimics what the natural is likely to do.

SUBSURFACE FLOATS. There are several ways to achieve this type of sub-surface float. An increasingly popular method is to attach a floating strike indicator about 2 to 3 feet above the fly. It lets you see the instant a fish strikes the fly, and it keeps the fly floating at the right depth, but it does look too much like a bobber for some tastes.

A more productive method would be to use an emerger or dry fly on a dropper rig. With this rig you fish two flies at the same time, a common tactic when classic wet flies were used extensively. When tying on a new piece of tippet material, instead of clipping the tag ends of both the leader and the tippet, leave the leader end about 6 to 10 inches long and tie your indicator fly onto it. As well as helping your pupa imitation float at the correct depth, you're fishing another fly that might well draw strikes.

A third method, especially effective for spooky or hard-fished trout, is to run a layer of paste fly floatant from the butt of your leader to a foot or two short of the end of your tippet. The floatant keeps the leader on the surface film, and the fly drifts along just below the surface.

INVESTIGATION AND OBSERVATION

Without becoming a scientific authority on caddis flies, how do you know which color and size pattern to tie on? The mayflies' regular progression of intense, short-lived hatches provided invaluable information. While there may be some overlap and a few times when more than one type of mayfly is on the water, that is rare. With caddis flies, multiple hatches are the rule, and predominant species can vary from state to state, and even from stream to stream. Which fly to use, then, is determined by personal observation and investigation rather than a generalized knowledge of the regular rhythm of hatch sequences, as it is with mayflies.

With caddis flies, you need to know which species is predominant in the stream and which fly is currently hatching. They are not necessarily the same thing.

When you use caddis larva imitations most of the time, as we discussed earlier, you should imitate the predominant species in the stream. That means literally looking for a specimen where you are fishing. Pick up a few rocks. Spend some time finding out what's in the stream. What you're looking for is that free-living worm attached to the back or bottom of a rock, or that net maker lodged down between a few pebbles, or the larva living inside the case.

Because caddis are prime trout food, it is important to identify the caddis types in a stream. Here Ed Lofland and his eldest son, Ron, examine cased caddis larvae in Yellowstone National Park's Lewis River.

As a general rule, the cased larvae will be much more brightly colored than the uncased larvae. Their cases of stream-bottom debris are their protective coloration. Open up a few cases and match your artificial to what you find, both in color and size. The free-living larvae that you find will more closely resemble the earthier colors of their habitat—the tans, browns, and olive colors. And you would much rather find these free-living larvae, because they are more readily available to the trout than the cased larvae, so keep searching for them.

In the process, carefully examine the cases to see if they contain the still active larvae or if they have been sealed off and the larvae have begun pupating. Certainly examine the pupae, for they might be nearing emergence, but remember that some caddis pupate for a long time. In fact some larvae seal off their cases in the spring and don't emerge until the fall.

For choosing pupal imitations, it is probably best to find a nearby adult. Because the rising pupae are really fully formed adults still within their pupal pouches, the colors of the adults will match the colors of the pupae. Yes, it is hard to capture an adult. They are agile runners and fliers. But check streamside cobwebs where they might have been captured, or the grill of your car, or the screen door of your camper. Or use an aquarium or butterfly net and scrape streamside bushes to capture a healthy adult. And then match your pupa artificial to the size and color of the body and thorax of the adult. Downplay the wing colors of adults because they are not as obvious in the pupal stage.

Should you go to all the trouble that caddis flies present? Only if you want to imitate the most abundant forage in a trout stream, proven to be the trout's favorite food. Yes, you should.

4
STONEFLY NYMPHS

It's easy to get excited about stoneflies. They are the biggest aquatic insects in flowing water, and the biggest fish in that water will rarely ignore them. In fact, several studies have shown that the larger the food item, the farther trout will travel from their holding lies to take it. So, where stoneflies are prevalent, our best imitation, barring evidence that the fish are focused on some other food item, is a stonefly nymph.

Note the two qualifiers in that last sentence. The first tells us to use stonefly imitations where stoneflies are prevalent, but stoneflies have the most rigid requirements of all aquatic insects for pure, well-oxygen-

ated water. And the second qualifier is that if trout are focused on some other food item, probably some form of caddis or mayfly, then their myopia and their holding position in the stream may mean they will either ignore your stonefly nymph imitations or not see them at all.

With only one or two exceptions, stoneflies, especially the largest species that we and the trout get most excited about, require pure, cold, rapid water to thrive. They are very particular about this, and wherever human activity has upset the purity of the water or the quality of the watershed, stoneflies tend to disappear.

Stonefly nymph imitations are big and meaty and attract the attention of good trout, like this healthy rainbow.

smother the eggs and nymphs of stoneflies. And relatively light pollution from agriculture, pesticides, or sewage treatment is lethal. Furthermore, the water must remain cold; 78 degrees F is about the maximum that stoneflies can endure. The biggest threat here is degradation of a watershed. When the protective, cooling shade of even the smallest tributaries and headwaters of a stream is removed, waters warm and become intolerable to stoneflies.

It is also important to note that stoneflies can and will return to a once polluted stream that has been cleaned up. A prime example of this is the Millers River in Massachusetts. During the first third of this century, the Millers ranked as one of the

The disruption to the original water quality doesn't need to be severe. Relatively minor siltation from logging, road building, ranching, or development activity can

On Maine's West Branch of the Penobscot River, Will Ryan has taken so many hearty river-run landlocked salmon on his stonefly artificial that the area has come to be known as Stonefly Heaven.

East's finest trout waters, its riverbanks literally crawling with stoneflies. Yet industrial and municipal pollution shut down the river in the blink of an eye. The effect of the enlightened push for clean waters in the 1960s and '70s stopped the pollution of this once fine river, and by the late 1980s, stoneflies, and the big trout that thrive on them, had returned.

It is little wonder then, that all serious anglers become tenaciously involved when their favorite trout streams are threatened, especially those rare gems that hold both trout and stoneflies. Those few that do remain need to be carefully guarded.

Where stoneflies and big trout do cohabit, the streams are inevitably breathtaking, both for the scenic natural beauty that their character demands and for the possibilities that await anglers. Steep hills and mountains surround stonefly water, and the valleys and ranges through which they flow are ruggedly challenging and always enticing.

Geographic Distribution

While our mind's eye usually focuses on those brawling, legendary rivers of the West when we picture stonefly water—rivers like the Madison, the Yellowstone, the Missouri, the Snake, or the Deschutes—stoneflies are truly transcontinental. They range from New England's strong rivers, like the West Branch of the Penobscot, the Upper Connecticut River, the Housatonic, and the Farmington, all of which have produced good catches for me on stoneflies, through the Adirondacks, the Catskills, and the Poconos, to the Upper Midwest and beyond.

Nonetheless it is hard to ignore the

Stoneflies thrive in cold, pure, well-oxygenated water, like this section of the West Branch of the Penobscot River in Maine.

vision of the vast hatches that come from the *Pteronarcys californica* stonefly nymph of the West, the salmon fly hatch. The appearance of these big, dark brown flies and their cousins the *Calineuria californica*, or big golden stoneflies, is the highlight of the western fly-fishing year, and anglers from across the continent, including me, will schedule their lives around them. They hatch in such numbers and are so big that even the largest trout become positively frantic to take them in.

This famous hatch keys to a water temperature of 60 degrees F and thus moves upstream as headwaters reach that temperature. Its intensity tells us that the nymphs, which live from two to four years underwater, are numerous and available to trout all the time. Rarely will an angler go wrong by tying on a giant Salmon Fly Nymph or a Golden Stonefly Nymph.

In the East and Midwest the corresponding big stonefly nymphs are *Pteronarcys dorsata* and *Allonarcys*, giant black stonefly nymphs, and *Neoperla clymene* and *Peresta placida*, which are a golden to yellowish color. The major difference between these species and the western stoneflies is that these species are largely nocturnal in their emergence and egg-laying activities, so that they're little noticed by anglers. But they rival their Rocky Mountain cousins in size and they are abundant, and therefore particularly important underwater food sources for trout.

There are, of course, many other species of stoneflies throughout North America. More than 500 have been identified. And some of these others can be important to anglers as the fish focus on them. There are two or three books that go into greater detail regarding species, namely Schwiebert's *Nymphs*, which devotes one chapter to them, and Eric Leiser and Robert Boyle's *Stoneflies for the Angler*. A fully detailed

book about stoneflies that would rival the work done for mayflies by Caucci and Nastasi's *Hatches* or for caddis by LaFontaine's *Caddisflies* hasn't been written yet. We can only hope that as anglers become more attuned to just how prolific and productive stoneflies and their imitations can be, some brave soul will undertake what will surely be a monumental task.

When to Fish Stonefly Nymphs

The life cycle of stoneflies is similar to that of mayflies, namely, egg, nymph, and adult. During the hatch the nymph usually climbs out of the water onto the stream bank or a rock, log, or bridge piling, where the nymphal shuck splits and the adult steps out. There are a few smaller species that do emerge at the surface of the water, but for the most part they are localized. Fishing dry-fly imitations, then, is usually limited to those few days when the females return to the water to deposit their eggs. Fishing nymphal forms of stoneflies remains productive for the entire year, but it becomes especially effective as the mature nymphs begin to reposition themselves and move toward the shores or the places where they will emerge from the water.

Stonefly nymphs have two other physical characteristics that anglers can take advantage of in fishing their imitations. First, they have rudimentary gills, usually found at the base of their legs on the bottom of their thorax. These gills are quite inefficient when compared with those of mayflies, and they offer a good explanation of why stonefly habitat needs to be so oxygen enriched. When a good stonefly river becomes murky or silted because of a downpour or a fast snowmelt or upstream dam releases, stone-

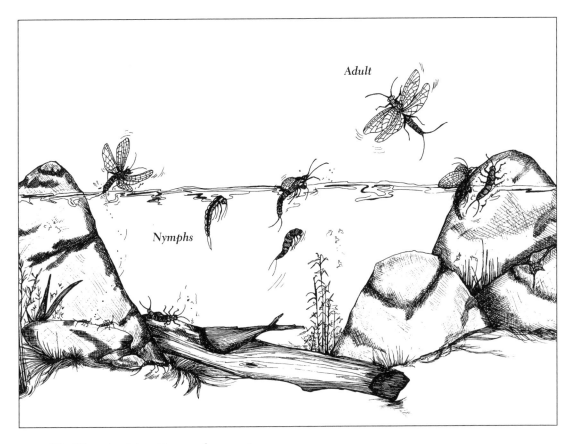

The life cycle of stoneflies runs from egg to nymph to adult. Most stoneflies crawl out of the water to hatch, so the time of their migration to shore is especially productive for fishing these artificials.

flies will often crawl up onto the top of stream rubble to increase the flow of water over their gills. In this position they are vulnerable both to direct trout predation and to being washed away. And the trout are especially anxious to take them.

The second characteristic that can help anglers is that stonefly nymphs go through so many molts. The largest nymphs may go through 30 or more molts before reaching adulthood. And when they step out of their old shuck, the color of their new one is very

light in the water, almost white. It takes several hours for this new shuck to regain the hardness and color of the old one. In addition, the process itself is dangerous to the insects because they often step out of the old shuck and directly into the current, floating along and vulnerable to trout until they can reattach to the streambed. Leiser and Boyle devote an entire chapter to "The Secret of the White Nymph," and Dave Whitlock in his chapter on stoneflies in *Guide to Aquatic Trout Foods* lists an entire series of lighter colors for imitating these molted stonefly nymphs.

Two other important pieces of information will draw anglers to productive stonefly water and help them decide when to use which artificials. First, there is a direct correlation between prey size and trout size. In streams that might have plenty of mayflies, caddis, and midges, but few if any stoneflies or other large forage, trout can grow to 10 to 12 inches long, but rarely bigger. The trout just don't have the nutritional intake to grow any larger. Where stoneflies occur, they can be 10 times larger than mayflies and will provide much more nutrition per food item. Will trout grow 10 times larger when stoneflies and other large forage are present? Maybe, especially if you consider that a 10-inch trout weighs ½ pound.

Behavioral invertebrate drift—when stream insects disperse within the natural flow of a stream—provides an exceptional time to fish underwater imitations, particularly in low-light situations.

Better forage provides the potential to produce a 5-pounder.

The second important bit of information involves what scientists call "behavioral invertebrate drift." This is a process of population dispersal that involves the predominant invertebrates in a stream—the mayflies, caddis, midges, and stoneflies. It is a conscious effort by the invertebrates to get up into the water column and drift with it downstream to new locations. It starts as the light of day dims and continues most of the night, and it is a daily event, particularly during the optimum fishing months.

Since trout are sight feeders, and since there is an abundance of subsurface food in the water column at dusk and dawn from behavioral invertebrate drift, swimming our imitations through good holding water at

those times makes most sense. Add to the equation the trout's propensity for taking the largest food item available, and you see the beginnings of a strategy—stonefly nymphs work well most of the time but are especially effective at dusk and dawn.

By pooling what we have learned about stoneflies, we can come up with a practical strategy for selecting imitations. Fish standard patterns of stoneflies when mature nymphs are positioning themselves to hike out of the water in anticipation of hatching. At dusk and early in the morning, these same mature imitations of big natural nymphs will work best, as they will in high murky water. But when we are using stoneflies as a searching pattern, when we don't have good reason to use the standard dark patterns, then lighter, just-molted colors are probably more productive.

Our efforts should follow the same timeline. If you have limited time or need to choose when to fish stoneflies, the best time is as the nymphs are moving toward shore, the next best time is at dawn or dusk, then when the water is murky. If you have the luxury of fishing at other times, tie on the molted patterns.

Stonefly Nymph Imitation

Because stonefly nymphs are large, some of our most innovative and skilled fly-tyers have been able to bring their imitations to nearly lifelike perfection. These creations belong in museums—or at least in frames for den walls or under glass domes for admiration—because of their beauty and because they aren't very effective at imitating the natural insects in the stream. To bring out the detail that attracts the human eye, the creators of these exquisite artificials must of necessity leave out the details that attract trout, the impressionistic materials that throb and move underwater to imitate vibrant, live insects. Out of water these materials just look messy. Underwater, however, they add texture and life to the imitations.

A good core of useful stonefly imitations focuses on the same details that make all artificial flies effective—size, color, shape, and movement. Size and color are the easiest to copy. The shape of the artificial comes under some debate among anglers, and the amount and type of material used to give the

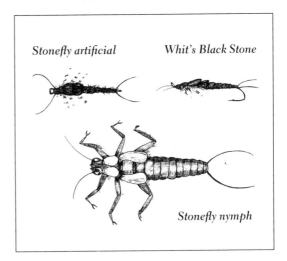

Stonefly artificial   Whit's Black Stone

Stonefly nymph

The Montana

artificial life and movement is usually a matter of personal preference.

Unlike imitations of other insects, stonefly artificials do not have universally accepted patterns that imitate particular species. Dry patterns of stonefly adults have been sorting themselves out some, with the Improved Sofa Pillow, the Yellow Sally, the Seducer, and Bird's Stonefly gaining acceptance as standard patterns. But there are only a few recognizable patterns of stonefly nymphs. Among them are the Montana (see illustration above), the Bitch Creek, the Girdle Bug, and, perhaps, the Wooly Worm. Yet these patterns are all more suggestive than realistic. They are relatively easy to tie, and they will take trout, but their imitative qualities are wanting.

Two famous angling writers addressed stonefly imitations in particular, although not at length. Polly Rosborough, in his book *Tying and Fishing the Fuzzy Nymphs*, devoted a chapter to stoneflies, and his "fuzzy" imitations emphasized slender, buggy-looking flies. Charles Brooks focused on two basic artificials, his Brooks' Montana Stone and Yellow Stone; their main feature was being tied "in the round," so that regardless of their position in the stream, they presented the same profile. His idea of creating flies that give the same impression regardless of their position is discussed at more length in Chapter 7.

Perhaps the most useful guidelines for creating specific artificials to imitate specific stoneflies come from Dave Whitlock in his chapter on stoneflies in *Guide to Aquatic Trout Foods*. His pattern is fairly standard for all the stonefly species, but he varies colors to match the naturals. His abdomens and thoraxes are tied with rough-blended dubbing to give a lifelike impression, and he uses soft but sparse hackles to imitate legs. Among the important details he includes are these facts: The underbodies of stoneflies are generally lighter than the overbodies, so he uses a darker shade of Swiss straw for the overbody, wing cases, and head. The gills of stoneflies tend to be very light, so Whitlock wraps light ostrich herl over the thorax before adding legs and tying down the wing cases. He is careful to rib the abdomen because the natural is distinctly segmented. And he weights his patterns so they will drift near the bottom. Specific tying instructions for his pattern are given in Chapter 14.

CORE PATTERNS

To get back to our core of imitations then, the following outline for a half-dozen patterns should help any angler meet most stonefly situations. The patterns should all be tied on 3X to 4X long hooks either with a straight shank to imitate stoneflies crawling along the bottom, or with the shank bent a bit in the middle. The bent-shank imitations are my personal preference because when the natural stonefly nymphs free-drift in the current, they bend into a semifetal position.

PATTERN 1. The first pattern imitates both the giant salmon fly nymph of the West and the giant black stonefly nymph found in the Midwest and the East. Tie it on large, size 2 to 6, hooks and make the dubbing for the thorax and abdomen brown to dark brown. The top of the fly should be black, the gills a light orange, and the legs a dark brown. Hen grizzly hackle dyed dark brown works well. Tails and antennae should be

An imitative pattern of the giant black stone-fly, Pattern 1.

dark brown to black, and the antennae should be a bit shorter than the tails.

PATTERN 2. The second stonefly artificial that no angler should be without resembles the golden stonefly nymph of the West and the more widely distributed orange stonefly. The western version is larger, tied on size 4 to 6 hooks, while the smaller version is well imitated with size 8 to 10 hooks, but they both follow the same color scheme. Use golden amber dubbing for the abdomen and thorax, a brown topping, and cream ostrich herl for the gills. Legs should be tan—standard grouse or partridge hackle works well—and tails and antennae can be light brown to orange. Antennae for these flies should be shorter and finer than the tails; woodduck flank feather barbules work well.

PATTERN 3. Pattern #3 imitates a number of brown stoneflies that are not nearly as large as the giant blacks of the first pattern. They are best tied on size 8 to 12 hooks. The abdomen and thorax are dubbed with a pure brown to lightish brown dubbing, but don't approach a tan color.

The topping for the abdomen and thorax is brown to dark brown, and the gills are cream colored. Legs are tied with the same brown hen hackle used in pattern #1, and tails and antennae are brown.

PATTERN 4. Pattern #4 uses a lighter amber dubbing than pattern #2 and is tied on size 8 to 10 hooks. The dubbing approaches a deep yellow in color and is overtopped with a brown to light brown Swiss straw. The gills are cream colored, and the tails and antennae are similar to the body in color, but on this pattern the tails should be a bit shorter than the antennae.

PATTERN 5. Pattern #5 tends more toward light amber to pale yellow, and it is small—size 10 to 12 hooks are about right. The dubbing is pale yellow but not quite cream. The gills are cream; the overbody is amber. Legs are pale yellow, and dyed grizzly hen hackle is the best material. Antennae and tails are also yellow, and dyed mallard flank works well.

PATTERN 6. Pattern #6 imitates those smaller olive green stoneflies that can often save the day during the height of summer and on into autumn. They're not large, tied on size 12 to 14 hooks, and the olive dubbing should be fairly light colored. The overbody should be a true olive to dark olive, and the gills are gray. Legs, antennae, and tails mimic the underbody color—pale olive.

For the molted versions of these six patterns, and for all imitations of molted stoneflies, Leiser and Boyle insist that an all-white artificial is the answer. Whitlock lists very particular, lighter colors ranging from a reddish brown for the Black Stonefly to light yellow and cream for the lighter Amber and Olive Stoneflies.

In fact, fishing with patterns that imitate

Will Ryan's impressionistic stonefly pattern emphasizes motion and lifelike qualities in its materials.

molted stoneflies is still very new, and much more observation and experimentation need to be done. Suffice it to say that patterns designed to imitate molted stonefly nymphs are certainly lighter in color than the standard ties, but they must still maintain the accuracy of all good artificials in size, shape, and lifelike qualities.

The half-dozen patterns listed in this chapter, and their corresponding light imitations, will cover the majority of instances where the water calls for stonefly artificials. The choice of which pattern to use and when to use it is almost always a matter of observing which stoneflies inhabit the stream and how abundant they are. The process is not difficult because most hatching stoneflies leave their shucks behind, out of water. And a few minutes of examining streambed rocks or seining a few samples of nymphs can pinpoint what's happening underwater and which artificial to tie on.

Stonefly Nymph Presentation

Stoneflies are almost always found on the bottom of the stream. They are poor swimmers. These two facts dictate that in most circumstances we need to fish deep and our flies should be dead-drifted with little, if any, motion.

Fishing stonefly nymph artificials deep and dead-drifted is easy to suggest, but it requires a good deal of experience and practice to accomplish. While all good stonefly water is well oxygenated, rarely will the stream in which we're fishing stonefly nymphs be uniformly fast flowing and rock strewn. Rapids, riffles, pocket water, pools, and a variety of depths will all be encountered, and often in just a short length of river. Because of this, there is no one sure recipe for constructing terminal tackle that applies to all water types in a single stream, let alone to the variety of rivers and streams where stoneflies are abundant. Our approach to each river and to each section of a particular stream needs to suit the water and circumstances we find there.

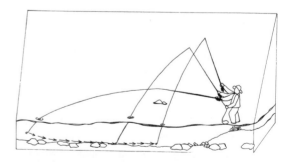

The upstream dead-drift presentation is ideal for fishing stonefly patterns because the insects swim poorly and generally just drift along until they can reattach to the streambed.

SINKING OR SINK-TIP LINES

Our first problem is to get the fly down to the bottom, and there are three different methods of doing so. First of all, some anglers prefer to use sinking or sink-tip lines for all situations. While there are distinct conditions where this is preferable, such as in broad, deep pools or backwaters or in other still-water situations, most of the time it is not productive because the fly line disappears under the water. Because the fly line is our only clue to what's happening with our artificial underwater, the more of the line we can see above water, the better. So, whenever practical, a floating line is preferable.

WEIGHTED LEADERS

The second method, preferred by many anglers, is to use some sort of weight attached to the leader, and in many instances this tactic works well. It is especially appropriate for a stream that contains a wide variety of waters because the weight, whether split shot, soft weight, or wrap-on weight, can be added to or taken off the leader easily, allowing an angler to match the circumstances he finds in each section of the stream.

Will Ryan, a longtime fly-fishing writer and fly designer, uses stonefly artificials extensively for trout, landlocked salmon, and, especially, smallmouth bass. His solution to getting his flies deep is to leave a length of tippet material dangling from the blood or surgeon's knot that connects his tippet to his leader. He ties an overhand knot in the end of the dangling material and adds his split shot to the extra monofilament. When the rig gets caught up on the bottom, as it will with frustrating regularity regardless of the method you use, pulling it free generally leaves just the weight on the streambed, not the fly. Another advantage of this method, as Will points out, is that you can construct the fly without extra weight, and while the tippet weight will bounce along the bottom, the fly will float just above it.

WEIGHTED FLIES

The major disadvantage to adding any sort of weight to the leader is that the weight interrupts the direct connection you should have to the fly. A fish picking up any artificial will quickly feel that its texture is not right and will try to spit it out. For consistent hookups, the angler needs to detect the pickup almost as it occurs so that he can set the hook. Certainly a fish grabbing a stonefly nymph will hook itself at times. But when the take is more subtle, that momentary pause in the movement of the line is our only clue, and we need to strike immediately. For this reason, our third method of rigging is usually the best, namely, a floating line with a leader length to match the water being fished, and a weighted fly.

By constructing the imitation with weight built into it and using the tippet and leader length to match water depth and velocity, the angler maintains direct control of his fly and can detect pickups more easily and set the hook more quickly. The downside, as we mentioned before, is that this is one sure way to lose flies. But the cost in flies will usually be more than offset by the quantity and size of the fish caught.

Once our fly is down on the streambed, it needs to drift free, with little motion or interference from the leader, line, or angler. As simple as this sounds, the variety of water and angling conditions we'll encounter on good stonefly streams requires a fairly extensive arsenal of presentations. Charles E. Brooks, in his books *The Trout and the Stream* and *Nymph Fishing for Larger Trout*, listed no fewer than 10 separate methods of presenting nymphs. He was a stonefly nymph specialist and used each method under separate, distinct conditions when fishing stonefly imitations.

Core Presentation Methods

For our purposes, two or three core methods will get us started, and as our experience accumulates, more subtle presentations will naturally evolve.

Upstream Cast

The most obvious presentation to ensure a drag-free drift is the straight-upstream or up-and-across-stream cast. I use this cast whenever possible, although the details of maintaining direct contact with the fly need careful attention. For the straight-upstream cast, the water depth and velocity dictate whether we can keep a straight, slack-free line between us and the imitation. This will become apparent after a few casts. Direct-upstream casts should be made only when we can easily keep ahead of returning line and concentrate on whether the fly has been taken by a trout.

Up-and-across-stream casts must likewise be long enough to allow the fly to get to the bottom, but we also must manage our fly line to keep drag from occurring while keeping direct contact. Because there are often conflicting currents, we'll need to mend the line either just before it alights on the water or soon thereafter. For me, this is the most difficult presentation, and I'll use it only when I can't position myself for a more direct-upstream cast.

Across-Stream Cast

A strong, hard current means that we probably can't make a direct-upstream or up-and-across presentation. Because of the speed and strength of the current, we would need to make a fairly long cast to give the fly enough time to get to the bottom, and we'd be forced to strip back line very quickly. Often, we'd be working so hard to keep the slack out of the line that we'd miss strikes. More appropriate for hard flows of water is positioning ourselves directly across from the good holding water and making the shortest possible across-and-upstream cast. We still want the fly to get deep, but our line management as the fly gets back to our target area and as it actually passes it will give us a much longer drift along the bottom.

With this presentation, we actually end up facing downstream, because the slack we've taken off the water, often by raising rod and arms over our head, can be fed back down onto the water as the fly passes by. My wife, Pat, has often chuckled to see me with my hands and rod up over and behind my head to control slack, only to get a strike just then. I apparently look like a fly-fishing contortionist when I try to set the hook, but the method works.

Downstream Cast

Each of these methods can be used when our strategy is to fish at dawn and dusk or to fish roiled, colored water, or when we're casting stonefly imitations as searching patterns. When we're intent on imitating stoneflies as they migrate to the shallows in anticipation of hatching, however, we'll want to give a bit more action to the fly. And to do this we'll need to cast straight across or across and downstream.

It's important to remember in this set of circumstances that because stoneflies don't swim well, the water that they are intent on reaching will probably be a bit less turbulent than where they have matured. It may even be calm. While they won't swim into this position on the stream, they do crawl well across the bottom, and we are trying to imitate these moving, crawling insects that often trigger excited feeding from the very largest fish. We are trying to get our imita-

With strong and conflicting currents, straight-upstream or across-and-upstream presentations work best in stonefly waters.

tions to resemble these migrating stoneflies, so a slow, sweeping, bottom-hugging, downstream presentation can be highly effective.

Stoneflies may be exciting, but they do present a variety of problems in imitation and presentation. Observing the naturals, however, and the way trout respond to them, make the task of deciphering their mysteries a labor of love. Learning how to tie and select appropriate artificials and how to present them in a lifelike manner is not only a strong reward in itself, but also the best way to drive even the largest trout in a stream to distraction.

Stoneflies can make excellent searching patterns because it is the rare trout that can resist the big meal they represent. This rainbow took a deep-drifted stonefly imitation in Slough Creek in Yellowstone National Park.

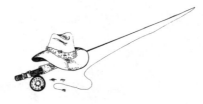

5
MAYFLY EMERGERS

As we've seen in Chapter 2, mayfly activity, and the way trout respond to that activity, depends on impending or in-progress hatches. When we're using nymphs down near the bottom of the stream, we need to know that the patterns we've tied on imitate nymphs that are in their longest instar (the last one before they hatch) and approaching the time of the hatch, because that's when they become active, move out of their hiding places, and are available to trout.

The Hatching Triangle

In the natural progression of the mayfly hatch cycle, from nymph to emerger to dun, the times when these food forms are available as forage can be seen as something of a triangle. At the base is the nymph on the bottom of the stream as it gets restless, begins to move about some, and then positions itself for its rush to adulthood. In the middle of the triangle, covering a shorter time span than the bottom nymphs, is the emerger se-

Emergers of the largest mayflies can bring the largest trout to feast on them, like this big brookie.

quence, when nymphs are actively seeking and eventually finding the surface. At the peak of the triangle is the time of the hatch itself, when duns are actually on the surface.

The triangle also signifies the relationship between the various phases of the cycle that are available to trout. Again starting from the base of the hatching triangle, nymphs are available throughout the triangle's entire time span. That means that even as emergers are rushing to the surface and duns are drying their wings, there are nymphs still available on the streambed.

As we go up the triangle to emergers, we see that they are available to trout for a shorter time than the streambed nymphs, but for considerably longer than there are duns on the surface. The emergers are also available before, during, and, to a degree,

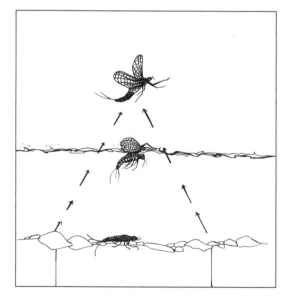

As a hatch sequence moves up the hatching triangle, the time covered by the phase of the hatch decreases but the intensity of the available food items increases, and trout will feed where food is most abundant.

after the duns have hatched. Only at the top of the triangle do we have the actual duns, and their time as available forage to trout is the briefest of all phases of the hatch.

If the nymphs are available throughout the hatch, and the emergers are available before, during, and after the duns, why should we ever fish anything but nymphs on the bottom? Why make the effort to imitate and fish emergers? And why fish a dry fly at all?

The answer to these questions is simply that the trout climb the triangle, too. They will indeed spend most of their time taking in the active nymphs on the streambed. They will spend less time concentrating on emergers. And they will spend the least time on the duns.

Trout follow the progression of the hatching triangle to take advantage of the feeding opportunities it presents. As the hatch progresses, and the length of time shortens on the way up the triangle, concentrations of insects increase. The density of food items is greater the closer we get to the top of the triangle. They are densest when the duns are all over the water.

The first idea this triangle should convey to the angler is that the amount of time he devotes to the patterns and presentations associated with a particular phase of the hatch should correspond to the duration of that phase. Nymphs on the streambed are available for the longest time, emergers for less, and duns for the least.

The second idea an angler should get from the hatching triangle relates to the density of insects. As the density increases, so will the feeding activity of the trout. Should we ignore duns on the surface? Certainly not, because just about all of the trout in the stream will be concentrating on them. Emergers? Right again. The density of emergers is high enough to excite most trout in a stream, and also brings their activity to near

fever pitch as they position themselves for the feast to follow. Nymphs? Trout are opportunists when they're on the streambed. Rarely will they ignore a recognized food item that floats into their feeding zone.

In the context of this book on underwater flies, then, the hatching triangle helps anglers understand just why it is so important to devote considerable time to nymphing and to learning about the patterns and tactics that make nymphing so effective, as covered in Chapter 2. The triangle also helps explain why, in the last 15 to 20 years, more and more emphasis has been placed on emerging mayflies. Because trout focus on emergers—both as they begin their ascent from the bottom and later, as they become concentrated in and just below the meniscus—fly fishermen should spend a proportionate amount of time on them.

As we've seen in Chapter 2, the nymphs of a particular species of mayfly become agitated and active as the time of year for their emergence approaches and as the time of day for their hatch draws closer. Throughout the year there is a regular progression of species displaying this activity, from Quill Gordons to Hendricksons to Cahills to Tricos; and many fine angling books, as well as our own personal observations, can help us decipher which flies will be coming off at what time of year.

More difficult, especially before the duns appear on top of the water, is knowing where the trout are finding their easiest meals. As a general rule, if we know, for instance, that the Hendricksons are due, then fishing Hendrickson Nymphs deep is our first step. This holds true for all the mayfly species. Stated another way, in the absence of evidence that trout are feeding on some other phase of the hatch, fish nymphs deep. The hatching triangle tells us that trout spend most of their time picking off nymphs from the streambed.

The trout's transition from bottom-floating nymphs to emergers is not abrupt, but it is almost always inevitable.

As the nymphs on the streambed begin ascending, the trout rise to them and assume new feeding positions higher in the water column to take advantage of them. So, too, should the angler change his emphasis from fishing nymphs deep to fishing emergers.

You can see when the trout have made their move, because they will be feeding right at or just under the surface. Flashes, bulges, and distinct rise forms tell us just where the trout are finding their meals. Watching a working trout, instead of getting a cast over him as soon as he's discovered, often makes the difference between getting him to take the artificial and spooking him back under the far bank. Seeing just where he's feeding is crucial. Just a flash of flank color or the quick blink of his white mouth means he's still feeding on emergers as they rise and is not yet concentrating on food in or near the meniscus. Watch more closely, however, and you'll usually find that he is definitely within a foot or two of the surface. Bulges of water mean that he's very close to the surface, but still feeding under it. And actual breaks in the surface film mean he's onto the attached nymphs or feeding just barely under the surface.

This last phase, when the fish are actually breaking the surface, can be especially deceiving as to whether they're on duns or emergers. If the mayfly duns are large, like the Drakes or March Browns, you'll see them being taken. If the duns are small, it's harder to tell.

But remember, the hatching triangle tells us that trout spend more time taking nymphs at the meniscus than taking duns from the surface. So until you see clear evidence that the trout have actually switched over to duns, you should stick with fishing emerger patterns in the surface film or just below it.

A wrinkle to the classic progression of trout from nymphs to emergers to duns is that often the trout won't switch to duns at all. If the supply of emergers is ample and they remain easy prey, trout will continue to feed on them right through the entire hatch. This explains why we often can't raise a fish with a perfect dry fly when we're seeing rises all over the place in among the duns. The trout have simply stayed on the emerging nymphs.

Mayfly Emerger Imitations

Two distinct types of emerger patterns are both effective when trout are keying on subsurface mayflies at or near the meniscus. The first we touched on in Chapter 2. They are the same nymph patterns that we used deep, but they are tied on light-wire hooks, without weight, and are designed to float in or near the surface film. The second imitates the insect at that instant when the dun (subimago) is trying to escape its nymphal shuck right in the meniscus. Normally I've found that the nymph patterns work well, but on many of my favorite eastern streams, hard-fished trout often need an extra triggering detail, and that's when I switch to the emerger patterns.

In the riffles of a stream, it can be difficult to tell whether the trout have actually switched over to taking duns from the surface. In the absence of firm evidence that they have, emergers will continue to produce well.

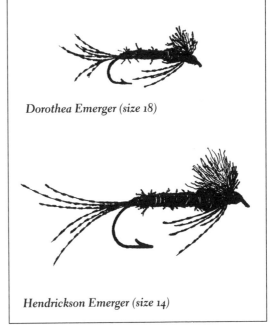

Dorothea Emerger (size 18)

Hendrickson Emerger (size 14)

CORE PATTERNS

The five nymphs listed previously will still serve as an excellent core of patterns for emergers: the Gold-ribbed Hare's Ear, the Hendrickson, the small Olive-brown, the Cahill type, and the small Black Nymph (see Plate 1). Any one of them, when matched to the active insect, will produce at or near the surface. But as anglers become increasingly attuned to the hatches and begin to understand some of the finer points of the information they provide (which mayfly species predominate at a given time and how their nymphs behave underwater), they may want to fine-tune their patterns and their presentation methods.

OTHER EMERGER PATTERNS

WIGGLE NYMPH. Doug Swisher and Carl Richards wrote an entire book devoted to emergers. In fact, that's the title — *Emergers*. In it they developed quite sophisticated patterns to imitate mayflies, especially swimming mayflies as they make their way to the surface. Their main contribution was the invention of the Wiggle Nymph. It is extremely realistic, but the price for this realism is the difficulty in tying it. A second hook, from which the bend and hook point have been clipped, is attached to the first hook with a hinge of strong tying thread, monofilament, or elastic.

Because of the hinge, as the fly is raised up through the water column in stop-and-go spurts, it mimics several of the strong-swimming nymphs found in the quieter stretches of streams. It is certainly a killer pattern for anyone willing to tie it, and is especially effective when strong-swimming nymphs — like Brown and Green Drakes, Hendricksons, Pale Morning and Evening Duns, and some of the smaller Blue-winged Olives — are imminent.

PHILOPLUME PATTERNS. Another innovative pattern uses grouse philoplumes to imitate the gills found along the bodies of many mayfly nymphs (see Plate 1). *Philoplumes*, the underfeathers from grouse body feathers, are like miniature marabou feathers. They are an almost perfect dun color and can add to a pattern the dramatic imitation of moving gills. The philoplumes are tied in by their tips at the bend of the hook, one on each side, and are brought up along the side of the abdomen after it is dubbed. The quills are tied off before the thorax is dubbed, and the ribbing material is wound through the plumes to give them gill-like separation.

Will Ryan, who is always investigating new ways of using fly-tying materials, first showed me the use of philoplume on his imitation of a potamanthus nymph. These big, slow-water, midsummer nymphs are particularly attractive to anglers because they are especially active for up to two hours before the actual hatch of the dun, commonly known as the Cream Variant or the Golden Drake. Because the dun inevitably does not emerge until after dark, it is easier to fish the nymph at dusk, and it is exceptionally productive. You can adapt this method to any of the larger mayfly nymphs that display distinct gills, like some of the Drakes, the March Brown, or even the larger Hendricksons.

SWIMMING NYMPHS. Both the Wiggle Nymphs and the philoplume patterns attempt to achieve a more lifelike action. An adaptation that's a bit easier to tie is the addition of a soft-hackle collar on many of the traditional nymph patterns (see Plate 1). Although most of these patterns incorporate a wing case and use a few fibers for legs along the bottom of the thorax, those features are eliminated in the swimming nymphs. The purpose of the hackle collar is to give more motion to the imitation, and

Emergers, when fished effectively up through the water column and just below the surface, will produce consistently and for longer periods of time than dry flies.

the elimination of the wing case and under-legs improves the attractiveness of the imitation regardless of whether it is floating sideways or upside down. The swimming nymphs and their evolution will be discussed more thoroughly in Chapter 7.

HATCHING NYMPHS

The second distinct type of emerger pattern imitates the nymph when its shuck is splitting and the dun is attempting to step out. It represents that troublesome time, for anglers and for insects, when water-breathing organisms become air-breathing, and when wet-fly fishermen become damp-fly or dry-fly fishermen. The struggle for the insect is critical, but the argument among anglers as to whether they are using wet or dry patterns is trivial. I include the pattern in a book on underwater flies because it is as rooted to the nymphal form as it is to the subimago.

This type of artificial is best used when medium to large mayflies are coming off the water because these bigger flies do not endure the struggle to break through the meniscus that the smaller flies do. Instead, their biggest problem is pulling their large bodies out of the nymphal shuck. Again, because of their size, the meniscus does not push down on their nymphal shuck as effectively as it does with the smaller flies' nymphs, so the larger mayflies often have trouble escaping the shuck. Many of them, in fact, never do escape, and they become inviting targets for the trout.

The best imitations of the struggling emergers are the standard nymph patterns on light-wire hooks, but with a clump of dubbing fur or synthetic yarn added to the top of the thorax. You're trying to imitate the unfurling wings of the dun, so you want to match the colors of the wings of the dun. The preferred position of the fly is with the wing clump out of the water and the nymph body in it, so apply some paste floatant to the clump.

The last artificial that can be important during the hatch imitates the dun that has fully emerged but has not made that final, full separation from its nymphal shuck. It would seem that the easiest way to imitate this phase would be simply to add a trailing shuck to the standard dry-fly pattern, and in a pinch, this can work. In fact, in my vest I carry two or three squares of different-colored fabric from discarded nylons, and I often attach a small piece to the hook to make it look like a trailing shuck.

But a more realistic impression would be achieved by clipping the hackle fibers from the side of a standard pattern so that it floats on its side with one wing on the surface. I've often done this, but the drawback is that I've now got a box full of mutilated dry flies. Again, add a piece of nylon stocking as a trailing shuck.

Swisher and Richards tied special flies to address this problem; they moved the duck-quill segments from the sides of their no-hackle duns to the top of the hook and added a trailing shuck of Antron. With the quill wings on the top, the fly floats on its side and the shuck trails behind.

Mayfly Emergers Presentation

As we discussed in the section on presentation in Chapter 2, fishing underwater nymph artificials is keyed to the type of nymph we're imitating, whether clingers, crawlers, swimmers, or burrowers, and the types of waters where they're found. That knowledge also helps us understand just where to concentrate our efforts when a particular hatch is due to come off. But if we give any action at all to the artificial as the nymphs approach the meniscus and attach to it, the action should be much more subtle than when the nymphs and fish are deep.

ARTIFICIAL ACTION

As the nymphs approach the top foot or two of the surface, we need to give little or no action to the artificial for two reasons. First, the trout working the top of the water column are there because they are actively feeding. They're already tuned in to the hatch at hand, and we don't need to get their attention as we did when they were feeding at random near the bottom.

Our task near the surface is to get our imitation within striking distance. This is particularly important near the surface and toward the top of the hatching triangle because food items there are more concentrated. If a trout has positioned itself near the top in a prime feeding spot, it's already looking for the nymphs we're trying to imitate and they are already plentiful. Our job is to position our imitation correctly, and because the trout is already accustomed to taking the naturals, any action we give to the artificial might trigger a rejection of it rather than a strike.

The second reason to give less action to the emerger artificial is that with the limited space we have to work with, the top foot or two of the water column or the surface itself, we don't have room to maneuver. It would be nice to think that we have absolute control over even minute movements of the fly out at the end of the line, but it is rare that the effect of moving water, 10 to 15 feet of leader, 40 feet of fly line, and 9 feet of fly rod will let us move a size 14 fly an inch and a quarter. And yes, the trout will pick up on whether the movement is an inch and a quarter or 3 inches. So for the most part, we'll let the materials that we've built into the fly give it lifelike qualities in the surface area of the stream.

Nymph Types/ Water Types

Knowing, as we do, that clingers are found in the fastest water in a stream, that crawlers usually like moving water but not always

In fishing emergers up near the surface, an upstream, dead-drift cast is usually most effective.

rapids, that swimmers are in that fringe of water types between fast and slow water, and that burrowers are slow- or slackwater dwellers, we need to approach each of these sections of a stream with particular presentations. Nymphs vary distinctly from one section of the stream to the next, and often from stream to stream, so we need to examine each of them separately.

Fast broken waters are home to the important clingers, the March Browns, Gray Foxes, Quill Gordons, and Cahills. These clingers don't swim well, if at all, so they should be dead-drifted up near the surface or in the meniscus. Because of the heavy flow of water, dead-drifting any imitation is, at best, difficult; positioning becomes important so that we can make short, accurate casts.

In this instance, it matters little where the trout are in relation to us, upstream, down, or across. In fact, the hard flows of water won't let us choose just any position in the stream, because wading into position

may be difficult. We just need to be relatively close to the fish. And the hard flow and broken surface of the water will effectively cloak our presence regardless of where we are in relation to the trout. What matters is that we can put our fly exactly where the trout will see it, because they have little time to find it, decide to take it, and attack. The casts must be short and accurate because the flow in these sections will quickly drag and pull on our fly. But if we put our artificial in the proper feeding zone, and there is no telltale drag on it, the rises and takes will be quick and violent.

The crawlers are the mayflies that inhabit what most of us believe are the most attractive sections of a stream to fish. They're the Hendricksons, the Sulphurs,

The most productive sections of the stream are often also the most difficult to fish effectively. Often a bit of action is required to make the artificial seem lifelike.

some of the Blue-winged Olives, and the Tricos. They live in the gentler-flowing waters—the riffles, runs, and pocket water, that are so inviting and seem easier to fish. Yet these waters place subtle demands on free-drifting imitations and present their own unique problems.

Because these waters do not flow as hard as the water where clingers dwell, we need to be more careful of our own position in relation to the trout. The broken surface and general stream flow still help keep us hidden from view, but not as well as before, so our casts need to be longer. Yet in this part of the stream, we still face the problem of multiple and conflicting current flows. When we lengthen our casts, we're setting ourselves up for fly drag.

For that reason, the best presentation is straight upstream or up and across stream. Straight upstream works best if the currents vary where the trout are holding. If we can get directly below the trout and position our-

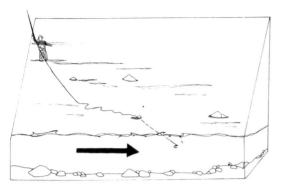

The up-and-across-stream presentation allows an angler to stay hidden from the trout in less turbulent water and yet still lets him present an artificial dead-drifted.

selves in the same current flow, then the fly and the fly line will be moving at the same speed, and the drift will be largely drag free.

The most common mistake in straight-upstream presentations is casting too far upstream. Because you are behind the trout, you're hidden, so you can get closer to the trout and make shorter casts. The longer the cast, the more probable that it will be too far upstream, showing the fish the fly line or at least the heavier butt section of the leader.

If the currents allow, make a reach cast from directly below the trout. If you bring the rod tip either to the left or right of straight upstream as the line stretches out in the forward cast, the downstream line will angle away from the trout's position. And even if the cast is a bit long, the fly line will be angled away from the trout's lie, and the fly will still float over him.

For the up-and-across cast when fishing the crawler nymphs, varying currents are always a problem. It's a rare spot in a stream that has a uniform flow from one bank to the other, so you must allow for faster and slower currents between you and the trout and your fly. In this instance, positioning is as important as always because you want

your fly line to cross as few currents as possible. Making a short cast up and across just one conflicting current is always better than crossing two or three different water speeds. Mending is almost always necessary, but mend with a purpose. Pay attention to the speed of the water you're adapting to and make larger or smaller mends as necessary. Again, the ultimate goal is to make your nymph or emerger drift without drag.

The swimming nymphs present two distinct problems. The small swimmers, the Baetis Blue-winged Olives in a variety of sizes from tiny size 24s to larger size 16s, are very active before emergence, but become almost inert when they get into the top foot or two of the surface. They demand dead drift. The large swimmers, the *Isonychias* and the *Siphlonorous* nymphs, in the #8 to #10 size range, prefer moving water and swim actively right up until hatch time. And it's important to understand that these large swimming nymphs actually hatch out of water, after they've crawled onto a rock or the shore. So stick with pure nymph patterns.

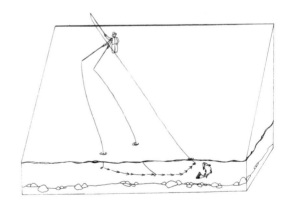

For the swimming nymphs, the Leisenring lift can work wonders. The angler needs to know exactly where the trout is holding so that he can raise the fly up in front of it to look just like an emerging nymph.

The small swimmers are most abundant in sections of the stream where the water has slowed, with glassy surfaces and conflicting, if nearly invisible currents. Because trout can see so easily in these conditions, these sections are the most difficult to approach and fish. Trout can and do cruise here, although they usually face upstream, so a longer cast is better, as long as it's a good one. Because of the easier flow, the conflicting currents won't immediately set up drag. And we don't want to be mending our fly line much because any surface disturbance is easily detected. A slack cast, then, from behind the fish or upstream and across, is perfect.

The large swimmers should be the easiest mayfly nymphs to use. Because they are in fast water, the angler is fairly well hidden, and because they do swim well in spurts, fly movement, even near the surface, is often an advantage. It is still important to keep control of the fly, so that the angler is putting some action into it and so that the fly is floating in the trout's exact feeding lie, but a bit of drag won't hurt. These flies can, like the clingers, also be fished from any position an angler can get into—upstream, across, or downstream from the trout.

The burrowers represent those major hatches that bring all the trout to the surface, and usually all the anglers to the stream bank. They are the Green and Brown and Yellow Drakes, the Michigan Caddis (yes, it is a mayfly), and the Golden Drakes. As in other hatches, but none more than these, the nymph just below the surface and the emerger pattern in the meniscus are often much more effective than the actual duns on the surface. For this reason, and because burrowers inhabit the slowest sections of water in the stream, good presentations on long lines with fine tippets are demanded. Specific location of the cast and the fly are probably least important with burrowers, because they take plenty of time to hatch and the water is slow, so the trout can move about to find their meals. The only time this doesn't hold true is during a particularly prolific hatch when lots of flies are drifting into a limited feeding lane. Then you must make pinpoint casts while still making delicate presentations.

This is the time when long casts are most effective because the angler is most obvious, but even in this very slow moving water, conflicting currents can cause drag. Drag will be a particular problem where flies are concentrated adjacent to stronger flows, so position well, usually downstream and to the side of the trout, and cast carefully either with a slightly slack line or with a reach cast.

It is again important to note that there are many excellent and extensive books on just which fly is hatching on what particular type of water. And many streams have such strong followings of anglers that hatching charts have been published for those specific waters. However, knowing the basics of the four types of mayflies, observing where they are hatching and when, and actually looking at one or two flies themselves can provide all the information an angler needs to tempt even sophisticated trout to take the fly.

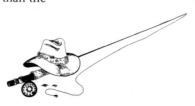

6

Caddis Fly Emergers and Underwater Adults

As we've seen, mayfly nymphs and emergers and caddis fly larvae and pupae at times occupy all of the underwater column. They can attract fish on the bottom of the stream, in the middle depths as they rise, and just below the surface as the nymphs or pupae rush toward the meniscus. It remains a fact, however, that the meniscus itself, that strange and sometimes impenetrable layer between the water and the air, is a very real barrier. For every insect living in the water and hatching on the surface, successfully overcoming the dangers of the meniscus is essential to achieving adulthood.

The barrier that mayflies and caddis flies encounter at the meniscus offers, quite simply, the best opportunity for trout to feed on them. Struggle as they must to break through it, the insects are trapped in a limbo between life and death. They are unable to detach themselves from the meniscus and flee to the bottom, and they cannot hurry the process of hatching, which includes breaking into the meniscus, shedding their nymphal case or pupal pouch, unfurling their wings, and flying away.

As we've seen, mayflies in this predicament overcome their vulnerability by hatching in short, intense bursts, with hundreds and thousands of individuals all rising to the

meniscus in a short period of time. And because the mayflies must dry their wings once
they are standing on the meniscus, the trout
do not need to feed in a frantic frenzy when
mayflies are in the surface film. They can be
more leisurely in sipping the duns that are
helpless to leave the surface until their
wings are set.

Caddis flies are another matter altogether. Because of that useful added phase
of their life cycle, pupation, once the adults
hit the air, it is a simple matter of trying
their fully formed and ready wings once or
twice and then flying off. The trout don't
have the leisure of sitting and sipping caddis adults. If they are going to get a meal

from hatching caddis flies, they must grab
them when they're available — during the
struggle at the meniscus.

Caddis flies at the meniscus face only
two outcomes: success or failure. For anglers, though, there are several degrees of
the success or failure, and several phases of
the struggle that can be imitated and used to
take trout.

To do that, we must understand the
struggle. For all caddis pupae, the rise
through the water column is often a struggle
in itself. Many pupae rise on their bubble
and use their legs to swim to the surface.
Sometimes this action gets them to the
meniscus on their first try; sometimes it
doesn't and they must return to the
streambed to reinflate their gas bubble and
try again. Regardless of whether they make
one or more attempts to get to the meniscus,

*The most vulnerable time for caddis pupae is
when they rise toward the meniscus, and trout
readily feast on them.*

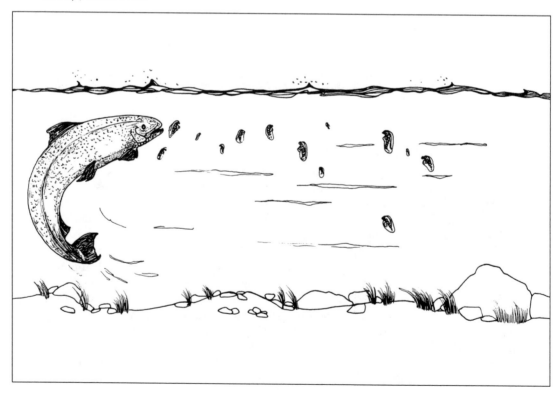

they are often exhausted when they do finally attach to it. Some may rest here for a few seconds before continuing the struggle, others may take a few to 10 minutes. And in this position, they are committed to continuing the struggle because the meniscus has now trapped them. They cannot disengage and return to the security of the bottom. They must either emerge as adults or die in the attempt. And this is when the trout feast on them.

Those flies destined to be successful have been helped by their pupal shuck to break through the meniscus, and it remains for them only to pull themselves up and out

Many species of caddis return to the streambed to lay their eggs; both descending to the streambed and returning to the surface, they are vulnerable to trout.

of it. Everything must go according to design, and every part of their body must be free of the shuck. If they clear it successfully, they need only an instant or two to try their new, fully developed wings and fly off. If things don't go right, the struggle continues and the fly often dies in the effort.

We may never know the scope of the problems that can doom a caddis fly at the meniscus. Possibilities range from nutritional deficiency in its larval stage, to pupal or larval injury, to injury at the surface because of swollen waters or unexpected turbulence, to chemical imbalances in the water, to atmospheric changes affecting the elasticity of the meniscus itself. But we do know that at certain times many caddis pupae don't survive the emergence process, and it seems that at all times some of them don't.

Damp Caddis Pupa Imitations

Anglers recognize two distinct types of underwater, or more correctly, damp, artificials that can be very effective when pupae attach to the meniscus during a caddis hatch. Each imitates a particular phase of the pupal struggle, and they imitate both successful and unsuccessful caddis flies.

The term *emergers* has come to be applied to any imitation that is fished in the meniscus. Yet as Swisher and Richards pointed out with their inventive imitations and in their groundbreaking book, *Emergers*, emerging naturals and their imitations are involved with every phase of the process of hatching, from the initial restlessness on the streambed, to the rise itself, to the activity at the meniscus. For our purposes in referring to flies at the meniscus, let's just call them *damp imitations*.

DAMP IMITATIONS UNDER THE MENISCUS

The first type of damp caddis artificial any angler should have in his fly collection may well be the most productive. It imitates the phase of hatching that every water-born caddis must go through, namely, attachment to

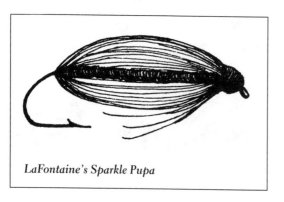

LaFontaine's Sparkle Pupa

the bottom of the meniscus. These artificials are designed to imitate the pupa before it has actually begun to escape its pouch. They are, for all intents and purposes, identical to the artificials we've used to imitate the rise of pupae from the bottom, except that they are not weighted and are tied on light-wire hooks. We want them to imitate the pupa as it rests on the bottom of the meniscus or when it is in the early stages of its struggle to escape its pouch.

LaFontaine's Sparkle Pupa (see Plate 2), when fished in the surface film, accurately imitates a pupa that has just attached to the meniscus. Use the same color schemes as for the Deep Sparkle Pupa, but omit the weight and build the underbody of fur a bit larger to replace the bulk of the weight. The synthetic fibers trap air and help the fly float, while the hook bend and point hold the fly down in the surface film. It floats right in the meniscus, just like the natural.

Older pupal patterns can also be used in imitating pupae attached to the bottom of the meniscus. The patterns highlighted in Solomon and Leiser's *The Caddis and the Angler*—the Fur Caddis Pupa (see Plate 2) and Solomon's Caddis Pupa—were both designed to be fished deep and moved toward the surface like emerging pupae. But again, if you tie them on light-wire hooks, they'll float in the meniscus and imitate attached pupae. If they do tend to sink, add a touch of paste floatant to their tops.

The Fur Caddis Pupa is easier to tie, having as it does just four basic ingredients: a fur body, a darker fur thorax, small dark duck-quill wings on the side of the thorax, and some guard hairs picked from the thorax for legs.

Solomon's Caddis Pupa uses the same fur body, but adds a rib to it, and uses the same fur for the thorax and the same type of duck quills for dark stubby wings. It adds the details of antennae and legs using par-

There are several exceptional caddis pupa patterns that work well, and large trout take them with confidence.

tridge or woodduck fibers and makes the head of the fly more distinct by using peacock herl.

For those of us anxious to use simple artificials to replace patterns that are more time consuming to tie, one of the best pupa imitations to use in the meniscus was first brought to my attention in Gary Borger's book *Nymphing*. He called it the Wet/Dry Fly (see Plate 2), and it is simplicity itself. On a light-wire hook, dub a fur body. Wind a soft hackle, which can be partridge or woodcock or starling, around the shank near the eye, tie it off, and you're done. Fish it in the meniscus as is, or add a little floatant. It has saved the day for me many times, and someday I may learn to tie it on first, not as a last resort.

No discussion of underwater caddis imitations would be complete without mentioning the work and attention that Jim Leisenring brought to the underwater flies he constructed with distinctly colored bodies and live-looking hackle. If his famous Leisenring lift is still on the tongues and in the minds of modern-day anglers, then his patterns should still be in their fly boxes.

Many of his artificials had the distinct profiles and colors of caddis flies because he tied them by imitating the naturals he found. He didn't have the detailed angling reference works that we do now, but he carried materials with him on the stream so he could immediately compare wetted dubbing to just-captured bugs. Many of his careful combinations of tying thread, dubbing, and hackle imitated caddis flies, and they are still effective artificials both down in the water column and in the meniscus. We'll cover Leisenring more thoroughly in the chapter on traditional wet flies.

Also of note is the reawakened attention that Sylvester Nemes has brought to soft-hackled flies. These flies are as old as fly-fishing itself, but they suffered greatly at the hands of the dry-fly euphoria that has gripped fly-fishing throughout this century. With his book *The Soft-Hackled Fly*, Nemes has brought these flies back to the consciousness of modern anglers.

Many anglers, like Pat, the author's wife, are genuinely surprised at the effectiveness of the ancient soft-hackled fly.

Simply put, soft-hackled flies (see Plate 2) are little more than bright, slim, floss bodies with a soft-hackle collar of hen feathers, partridge or any sort, giving a lifelike quality to the artificial. Some folks add a wisp of dubbing for a thorax. Their inherent bugginess makes them always attractive, and many of us find them to be excellent caddis imitations, again both in the water column and in the meniscus. More detail on their history and utility will be included in the chapter on traditional wet flies.

DAMP IMITATIONS ON THE MENISCUS

The second distinct type of damp imitations that often attract the attention of very selective trout are the flies that look like adults just stepping out of their pupal pouches onto the surface. In my experience, the key to this phase of the caddis hatch is the trailing shuck. Certainly the artificial has to maintain the impression of life, so the pattern has to maintain its sparkle and color. But the real insect, once clear of its pupal shuck, quickly flies away and is a difficult target for trout. Only when it is still attached to its shuck and anchored to its watery former life is it vulnerable.

Again, LaFontaine addressed this phenomenon with his Sparkle Pupa Emerger (see Plate 2), which is similar to the regular Sparkle Pupa, with its Antron pouch, but adds a few strands of Antron trailing behind the fly and includes some short deer-hair fibers for wings, which stick up above the surface. The head of the imitation is peacock herl.

Solomon and Leiser also broached the subject of the adult trying to emerge from its pupal pouch. They used standard-color fur bodies on light-wire hooks and added a short bunch of deer hair to the top of the fly's head. They included a few fibers under the throat of the hook for legs and used a paste floatant on the deer-hair wings to keep the body suspended down in the water and the wings above it. Again, a few wisps of synthetic fibers trailing off the back of the hook add to the impression of a trailing shuck, but this was not part of the original pattern.

A good argument could be made for simply adding some synthetic fibers as a trailing husk to any of the floating pupal imitations discussed in Chapter 3. The imitations from Solomon and Leiser, when dressed on light-wire hooks, would be especially effective with added trailing fibers. They were originally tied to imitate the caddis fly as it appeared in the pupal pouch, so their immature impression would be just as effective as the immature adult working to get out of the pupal pouch.

As good an argument could be made for adding a trailing shuck to any of the adult caddis fly imitations. They would represent fully emerged adults that couldn't get away from their own pupal shucks and were lying on the surface, exhausted or dead. In this case, shortening the part of the artificial that represents the wings would be beneficial, and eliminating any of the hackle fibers tied onto the adult imitation to get it to float on top of the meniscus would add realism.

Trailing shucks are often an indicator to trout that a caddis adult has been unable to escape its pupal shuck and is an easy meal. The author took this brown from the Beaverkill using a trailing shuck.

Underwater Adult Imitations

The distinction between adults stepping out of their pupal shuck and drowned or drowning adults may seem minor, but in certain instances the fully emerged adult, wings unfurled and often splayed in the water (and on it), draws very deliberate strikes from trout. This target is certainly the most highly visible and obviously vulnerable of any phase of the caddis life cycle. They are very attractive prey.

DEAD OR DYING ADULTS

Unexpected turbulence or high waters seem to injure more adults than pupae, so there are more angling opportunities with dead or dying adults. Particularly where the water is rising quickly, after a storm or below a dam during a release, the added gush and its unexpected depth seem to cause many caddis-adult casualties. Natural, hard, strong flows will also make a drowned-adult pattern effective.

In this situation, the patterns that work reverse what we were trying to accomplish with the damp patterns. We're trying to represent a fully formed, dead adult that is very often washed down into the water below the meniscus. Instead of trying to get a standard subsurface imitation up onto the meniscus, we're trying to get a standard floating pattern to drift along just below the surface. We avoid the materials that cause dry-fly patterns to float, materials like deer hair, stiff hackle, and buoyant synthetic fur; but the profile, color, and size of the artificials should still imitate the adult.

The best patterns for this situation would be adults tied with hackle-tip wings in the spent position, like the Delta Wing Caddis, or any of the patterns tied with turkey- or duck-quill wings, replacing the dry-fly hackle with soft, webby wet-fly hackle. Tie them on standard wet hooks to get them into the surface or just below it. A trailing shuck sometimes adds a little more attractiveness.

RETURNING EGG-LAYING FEMALES

The last phase of underwater caddis imitation that we need to address is the returning egg-laying female. Caddis flies are unique in that many, but not all, females carry their fertilized eggs to the stream bottom, attach them there, and then return to the surface. Some females gather on an exposed rock in the stream, or on the shore, and literally walk down into the water, while others dive directly into the flow. When they have finished their chore, they detach from the bottom and float and swim to the surface, where they break through the meniscus and fly away. Because of their long

Caddis adult females often gather on preferred stream-bank rocks or vegetation and then purposefully walk down into the water. Be sure to check for them; then match their size, color, and profile.

adult-stage lives, which can reach two weeks or more, the females can return time and again to the streambed.

Two important visual attractions draw trout to underwater adult caddis. The first is the flashy, alive look of the females. Because their wings are covered with tiny hairs (versus the scales or "dust" of moths), when the females submerge they take their air with them in the form of bubbles caught in these hairs. This trait allows the females to stay underwater for up to an hour as they lay their eggs, absorbing oxygen from the air bubbles on their wings. And the air bubbles glistening underwater draw the trout.

The second visual attraction of underwater females is their movement as they try to recover the surface. The single set of legs that served many of them so well in swimming their pupal shucks to the surface is now tripled. And when they head for the surface with their six legs flailing, their rise is, at the very least, active and purposeful.

The look of an adult caddis swimming through the water column certainly adds credence to the effectiveness of traditional wet flies presented in the standard down-and-across method. As the females struggle toward the surface, they are at the whims of the current, just as wet flies cast across the stream gain their action from the whims of the current.

So, many of the old standby quill- or flank-feather wing imitations are extremely effective pattern choices. If you are trying to match the natural, look at wing color and veining, and at the color and size of the body. Black, gray, or white duck quills are often called for, but the variety of colors and patterns in turkey tail or wing feathers can be more appropriate. Body colors are the same as in the pupal and damp patterns, cream to bright green to olive to brown to black.

The new synthetic materials can add a dash of flash to the wings. The Antron fibers from LaFontaine's patterns or Creylon or Z-lon fibers—used exclusively as winging material or a few of them added to standard wings—effectively imitate the flash of the female's wings or, more precisely, the air bubbles caught there.

To recap, then: At the meniscus, where trout do most of their feeding on caddis flies, pupal imitations stuck to the bottom of the surface film and emerging patterns imitating adults trying to free themselves from their pupal shucks are deadly. Fish them during the caddis fly hatch. Also during the hatch, drowned adults fished just below the surface can be the main attraction. At other times, returning female adults can be the only food item that will draw a trout's attention.

Caddis Fly Damp and Underwater Adult Presentation

The frustration most anglers experience when trout are keying on any caddis phase stems from the fact that adult caddis flies aren't nearly as obvious as mayflies. They don't usually hatch in uncounted numbers, although they can, and they don't wait around on the surface like mayflies. Without that major visual attraction, many anglers feel cheated. If there isn't the regular rise to nearly helpless duns, how can you possibly know when to fish caddis imitations? Since the caddis can't be easily gathered and inspected, how can you know which artificial to use?

In addition, a caddis hatch usually lasts longer than a mayfly hatch—each day and in total number of days. There is no brief, frenzied rise of flies and trout. Caddis are more casual, if no less important to the trout and the angler. No one I know has ever frantically driven to the stream bank, concerned that it's 3:00 P.M. and not 2:30, to meet the start of the grannom caddis hatch. They have for the Hendrickson. But caddis hatches are not the awe-inspiring events that mayfly hatches can be, and they can frustrate both newcomers to fly-fishing and veterans alike.

Yet it is expressly the length of the daily emergence and the number of days in a caddis fly hatch that should appeal to anglers. They don't need to rush into the stream, hands shaking, frustration rising as the

clinch knot slips, worried that the hatch will end before they can cover even one rising trout. They can relax—the fish will stay on the caddis, and the caddis will keep coming up. You just need to know what to look for.

You won't see thousands of insects floating along, but there are distinct, if subtle, clues that caddis flies are the primary prey on any given day. Anglers attuned to these visual subtleties can enjoy the productive casting of caddis imitations all day long. And choosing appropriate imitations, while not as simple as checking the chalkboard at Orvis, is not difficult.

Solutions to the two problems of choosing the correct caddis pattern and then fishing it effectively must be actively pursued by anglers. They must consciously watch the water for rising or feeding trout, identify rise forms or lack thereof, and search out specimens of the flies they need to imitate.

As we emphasized in Chapter 3, an angler intent on taking advantage of caddis activity must look for the type of fly the trout are

In numbers, caddis easily rival any other invertebrate in a stream, but they are much less noticeable. This New Hampshire flow, Perry Stream, produces strong, season-long hatches of caddis.

keying on. With larvae and deep pupae, you need to literally get your hands wet. With damp imitations and adults, you need to physically look at an adult. To do so, be persistent. Look for adults in streamside vegetation. Check eddies and backwaters for drowned adults. Use your aquarium net. Pump some trout stomachs. Rarely are there shortcuts.

Once you've determined the size and color of the imitation you are going to use, you must decide where and how to fish it, and this will further help in deciding which pattern to tie on—pupal, emerger, drowned-adult, or returning-female. Again, as noted in Chapter 3, when nothing is showing on the surface, go deep. But when there are fish obviously working in or at the surface, and there isn't an obvious mayfly hatch, watch carefully for the type of rise. It will help you determine what the trout are taking. If you see bulges of water, or casual rises, the trout are probably keying on pupae on the bottom of the meniscus. If the rises are more determined, even splashy or showy, the emergers (adults nearly escaped from their pupal shucks) are probably called for. After the hatch has been in progress for some time, and as the surface activity subsides, try drowned-adult patterns.

Only with returning adults do you need to look outside the hatching activity. And then you need to literally watch for adults intent on returning to the streambed. Luckily, it seems that females who are ready to stroll down into the streambed to lay their eggs have favorite gathering spots. If you see a few congregating on a rock or other surface rubble, some of them are probably scooting down into the water. At other times, as you watch the typical erratic flight of an adult over the water, you may see her plunge down into the stream and disappear. In either case, active-adult patterns are called for.

Fortunately for us, three of these four types of caddis imitation are often best fished

dead drift, right in the surface film. There are, however, some important exceptions. Only with returning adults do we always need to impart action to the fly, and even then the most productive presentation is the standard wet-fly, down and across drift.

STRAIGHT-UPSTREAM OR UP-AND-ACROSS-STREAM CAST

With floating-pupa, trailing-shuck, and drowned-adult imitations, the easiest and often most productive presentation is the straight-upstream or up-and-across-stream cast. It's very similar to dead-drifting a deep-running larva or pupa imitation in that you don't want the fly to drag at all. But it's unlike fishing deep imitations in that you don't need the straight line for direct contact with the fly. You'd prefer a longer drift, so it helps to throw some slack into your cast, either by overpowering it so it snaps back some or by wiggling the rod tip a bit on the forward cast. You use the bulge or splash of the trout as your visual strike indicator since the fly itself is difficult to see. And this means you need to concentrate on where you think your fly is floating.

One or two wrinkles in this presentation can help bring shy or extra-wary trout to the

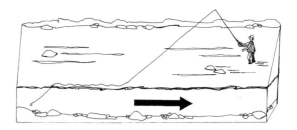

For returning female caddis diving into the water, an up-and-across-stream presentation works well. The trout may take the artificial either on its downward drift or as it rises at the end of the drift.

fly. Because the pupae and emerging adults are often actively trying to escape their shucks, a small bit of motion won't hurt. It has to be subtle, so try a cast or two with a straight line and use short (2 inches or less) strips of line to give the artificial some motion. And since some pupae near the surface actually swim toward the shore or toward rocks or logs sticking out of the water, the motion of a pupa imitation as it skitters along the surface film toward shore at the end of its dead drift can be a strong trigger for a trout strike. So don't pick up your fly too soon. Let it sweep across the current. This rarely works for emergers, but on occasion, for no good reason, it will.

Even for drowned adults, which would seem to demand nothing but a dead drift, the sweep at the end of the cast can produce well. Why? The drowned imitation immediately comes to life, like an underwater female, and attracts trout. In fact, it is probably impossible for trout to tell the difference between a dead adult, a dying adult, and an active egg-laying female, which often just drifts in the current. And the truth is, the trout don't care. It's a meal.

DOWN-AND-ACROSS-STREAM CAST

For live underwater adults, there are at least two distinct methods of presentation. The first is the standard down-and-across searching method. Cast the fly across and downstream and let it sweep across the current. Cast it farther upstream to get it deeper, and farther downstream when the water is shallow and riffley or slow. Impart a little drift and swim motion now and again by lifting the rod tip and dropping it back down. You can cover

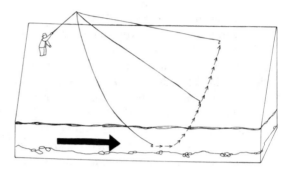

Adult underwater caddis can be presented with the downstream wet-fly swing. It's also an excellent method for covering water and prospecting for trout.

good lengths of stream with this method, and it is especially attractive when you aren't sure where the trout are holding, or, better, on a fertile stream with plenty of trout.

THE LEISENRING LIFT

The second method is the Leisenring lift presentation discussed on page 65. You want the fly to rise up through the water column in front of the trout. You need to see the trout or know where there is usually a trout holding, and you need to position yourself carefully so that the timing and location of your fly's rise are perfect.

Caddis flies spend a large proportion of their time underwater, as deep larvae or pupae, as rising and emerging flies, and as returning, egg-laying adults. Because they are so abundant, and because trout feast on them to such an extent, learning how to take advantage of all stages of caddis fly activity quickly results in more and better catches.

7
Swimming Nymphs

The serious study of aquatic food for trout during the last 50 to 60 years by dedicated angling investigators like Preston Jennings, Art Flick, and Ernest Schwiebert; more recently by Gary LaFontaine and Al Caucci and Bob Nastasi; and by a host of others has given the angler strong and varied reference works from which to identify which bug the trout are keying on in almost any given stream at almost any given time, and to pinpoint its family, genus, and species. They have also given us a good idea of exactly how the underwater forms of these insects — the nymphs, larvae, and pupae — live and move about. We know the water types pre- ferred by most species of mayflies, caddis flies, and stoneflies, and we're even fairly well informed about what they eat and how good their sex lives are.

Moving hand in hand with this entomological information boom has been the development of artificial-fly-pattern techniques and hypotheses. Yet the theory and practice of fly imitation have remained an inexact science. Expert and imaginative flytyers have brought their art to unimagined levels of precision. At least for the human eye, it is often difficult to tell a detailed mayfly or stonefly artificial from the real thing. But more and more anglers have dis-

Movement

covered that these perfect duplications of naturals lack some triggering mechanism that will cause the trout to inhale them as if they were, indeed, the naturals. Nowhere is this more evident than with underwater insects and their corresponding imitations.

A lifelike movement to the insect body itself, as well as effective manipulation of the artificial within view of the trout, is at least as important as size, shape, and color. It is now a well-established fact that a quality of motion, or some supple, throbbing, life-simulating material, must be incorporated into the construction of artificial flies to consistently fool trout.

Fly-tyers are increasingly aware of the need to consider the quality of lifelikeness in the materials they use, in addition to size, shape, and color.

The idea that an artificial must simulate the movement of life is, of course, not new. The very beginnings of fly-fishing centered on *moving* a fly through the water to attract trout. The oldest patterns were hackled and winged so that when an angler cast them downstream and across current, the flies would create the illusion of life. The rigid wings and often gaudy body materials did not in themselves add to the vitality of the imitation. The illusion was created largely by the movement across the water of the entire fly.

As fly-fishing attracted a larger core of innovative enthusiasts, especially in the late 19th century, it seems as if the entire body of anglers shifted toward imitating duns and floating adults. New theories of impression

and presentation emphasized the hapless floating insects that trout binged on when they were available. And this new emphasis is really what started the ball rolling toward the study of the insects themselves. After all, to get trout to take essentially motionless, floating artificials, you had to focus more closely on size, shape, and color. Because the flies either sat immobile and dried their wings on the surface or returned to the surface only to mate above it and die, lifelike movement was not needed and was rarely addressed.

Only when anglers again became interested in the subsurface lives of insects and trout did the pendulum begin to swing back to subsurface imitation and presentation. G. E. M. Skues pondered subsurface insects and their accurate imitation early in the 20th century and is probably responsible for the renewed interest in the subject. Other luminaries built on Skues' foundation, namely, that famous river keeper Frank Sawyer, and such other angling investigators as, again, Jennings, Flick, and Schwiebert. To that list can be added the careful watchers of their streams—Leisenring, Ovington, Swisher and Richards, Whitlock, Borger, and many others. But the foundation of their investigations was the imitative precision of the dry-fly masters who directly preceded them. Although many approached the subject of lifelike motion, it was usually through presentation, rather than through the alteration of their patterns. They diligently searched for materials and techniques that would more accurately imitate the bug's appearance, rather than searching for materials that would give the bug that fourth dimension—the aspect of life.

Adding the quality of lifelike action to imitations has not been entirely overlooked, however. Jim Leisenring, in the middle of the century, worked hard at matching his dubbing and tying thread, when wet, to the image of the natural underwater. His most enduring patterns used soft hackle around the shank of the hook near the eye, and his flies often had no wings or wing cases. Four of the five Leisenring patterns in Stewart and Allen's recent *Flies for Trout* were tied this way. But because of the lack of entomological studies at that time, Leisenring's flies are not directly related to specific nymphs. Nevertheless, they remain effective and popular.

Likewise, the patterns that have been touted for so many years by Sylvester Nemes, his soft-hackled flies, are productive largely because of the underwater movement of their soft-hackle collars. These patterns, like the Partridge and Orange and the Partridge and Green, were created hundreds of years ago, but they still work well. Why? It must be because the slim profile of their bodies is nearly overwhelmed by the action of the hackle. While a few writers have suggested that these artificials might imitate caddis pupae coming to the surface, that would be an accident of the pattern, for the flies offer only the faintest suggestion of the naturals.

Orientation

Charles E. Brooks contributed the idea of tying imitative patterns "in the round." His Brooks' Montana Stone and Brooks' Yellow Stone (see Plate 4 and the illustration on page 82) use palmered hackles and ostrich or peacock herls on the thorax of the imitations to suggest legs and gills regardless of the position of the fly as it drifts in fast stonefly water. Brooks lived in West Yellowstone and loved fishing for big trout in big waters with big flies. While the naturals he was imitating had a mildly flattened shape, Brooks relied on the motion of the hackle and herl and the lifelike quality of his fuzzy yarns to entice trout.

Brooks' Montana Stone, tied in the round.

By extending Charles Brooks' logic a bit further, and from my own streamside observations, two important and obvious bits of information emerge. First, when we are fishing underwater nymph imitations, we have little or no control over the fly as it dead-drifts down through the current. Once we've completed the cast and worked hard to mend the line so that the artificial is free from any influence of the leader or line, the fly is completely at the whim of the flowing water. It can ride upside down, backward, or on its side.

Second, the natural live insects don't do that. Certainly they might take a spin or two when some gush of water dislodges them, but invariably and almost immediately they will right themselves, and in fact will usually face upstream as they drift along. They, like every other living creature in the stream, and out of it for that matter, know instinctively which way is up. They'll have their back facing the sky and their legs ready to grab the first solid object they can find on the streambed.

If trout have been feeding on a particular nymph regularly delivered to them by the drift, invariably upright and obviously alive, then our most realistic artificial, if it lacks the correct position and a lifelike impression, will be allowed to float on by.

This extra selectivity, most anglers felt, was apparent only in streams that received heavy angling pressure, where the trout had quickly become leery of anything that even remotely spelled danger. But studies are now showing that trout must maintain the delicate balance of the energy equation and don't have the luxury of testing everything that floats by. They must eat what they know to be food. Both of these facts, the risk of danger and the energy equation, will cause trout to ignore imitations that don't float correctly and don't seem lifelike.

Our job, then, is to create flies that not only imitate the natural's size, shape, and color, but move with the vitality of the natural and either float upright all the time or eliminate the reference to their top and bottom. For underwater flies that we manipulate, that is, that we actually swim through the water, wing material forms something of a keel to keep the fly upright. This traditional wet-fly design, and how it can be adapted to current entomological information, will be discussed more thoroughly in Chapter 10. For dead-drifted nymphs, our best tactic is to eliminate the artificial's built-in reference to top and bottom, to tie the flies in the manner of Leisenring, Brooks, and Nemes.

Swimming Nymph Imitations

It may sound simplistic, but I think that many nymph imitations can be improved by eliminating the wing case and adding a collar of soft hackle. I know that this is true with three of my five core mayfly nymphs

Even in the slow pace of frigid waters, insects that become dislodged will right themselves. That's why swimming nymphs are a necessity, especially where selective trout prevail.

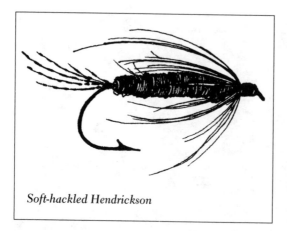

Soft-hackled Hendrickson

them in tandem, one fly on the end of the tippet and the other as a dropper. I switched them often so that they both had the same chances in either position on the leader. And the swimming Hendrickson Nymph outperformed the standard by 10 to 1.

It is important to note that I tried the same experiment during that same week with several other nymphs—namely the Hare's Ear Nymph, the Pheasant Tail, and the March Brown—and got similar results, with the soft hackles outcatching the standard ties by a substantial margin. Moreover, the Hendrickson patterns outfished the others by an even wider margin.

These experiments indicate that our fly selection should be based first and foremost on our knowledge of what's happening in the water. Our streamside observations are critical, too, and current reference books provide additional information we can use

A dropper setup.

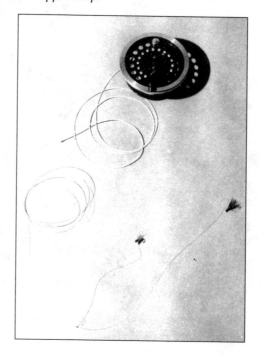

listed in Chapter 2 because I've experimented with them. With the Hare's Ear Nymph, the Hendrickson Nymph, and the Cahill Nymph, simply tying a collar of a single wrap of partridge hackle and leaving out the wing case has improved my catch rates. It is still important to match both the look of the natural we're trying to imitate and its behavior underwater, but the elimination of the top and bottom reference of the wing case and the addition of motion increase the attraction of the entire fly.

I recently experimented with the Hendrickson Nymphs for an entire week on that famously fickle water in Vermont, the Battenkill. I had been casually trying a few ideas on several of New England's more productive waters for a couple of years. Like many other anglers before me, I have always tinkered with fly patterns and now find myself leaning more and more toward moving, lifelike materials in all my subsurface flies, including nymphs, wets (see Chapter 10), and streamers (see Chapters 8 and 9).

When the duns were on the surface, I fished dry. However, during the hours before the hatch came off, I fished with subsurface Hendrickson Nymphs, using standard wing-cased patterns as well as a fly with a soft-hackle collar and no wing case. I fished

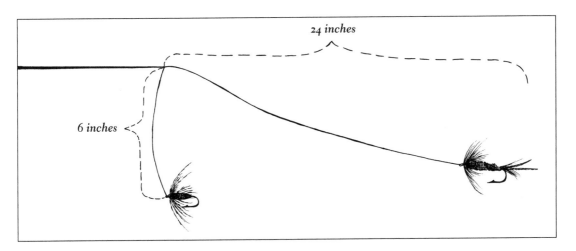

Note the distance from the dropper leader to the tail fly and the length of the dropper leader.

to identify the insects that are most active and available in the water. We still need to rely on proven patterns that have been developed over the years to imitate particular nymphs in particular situations. We then need to produce an underwater imitation that matches the size, shape, color, and action of the natural that predominates at the time we are on the stream.

Classifying mayflies as crawlers, clingers, burrowers, or swimmers, according to their type of activity (as we did in Chapter 2), helps us determine how much we should emphasize motion in the imitation. We can then decide how long the barbules of the hackle should be for our collar, how subtle or exaggerated the collar should be, and whether it might be more effective to palmer some short, soft hackle or herl onto the thorax.

Adding Motion and Light

These are my basic guidelines for adding soft hackle to nymph imitations: For crawlers, like the Hendricksons and Pale Morning or Evening Duns, the added collar

should be relatively sparse but should extend a bit past the thorax. For clingers—those flies that don't swim well and have a blocky, buggy-looking body often imitated by Hare's Ear types of nymphs—palmering some short hackles or ostrich herl over the thorax adds motion. Burrowers swim well and are usually large, so ample and long soft hackle at the eye helps. And swimmers, which can dart about quickly, need fairly heavy hackling, say two or three wraps, extending almost the length of the thorax.

When selecting soft hackle to wind onto the fly, choose it according to the look of the legs of the natural. A good aid here is to use a soft-hackle feather with markings similar to what the listed patterns use for legs at the throat of the hook. For example, the Hendrickson uses well-marked partridge or grouse hackle, while the Zug Bug uses brown hen hackle. When in doubt, refer to the natural and imitate its legs.

Certain nymph imitations are popular because their materials incorporate the light refraction and motion that are essential to imitating life. The Hare's Ear certainly qualifies because of the buggy, alive look of its coarse fibers. Nearly any fly with peacock, ostrich, or pheasant herl has a distinct iridescence and movement. The Zug Bug, which imitates the *Siphlonorous* and *Isonychia* nymphs, falls into this category, as does Charles Brooks' Ida May, an imitation of the western Green Drake Nymph. Brooks tied this mayfly nymph imitation as he does his stonefly nymphs—in the round, with peacock-herl ribbing along the entire body and dark green grizzly hackle encircling the front of the fly. Even a tiny well-tied Brassie has a turn or two of peacock herl for its head. And the revered Pheasant Tail Nymph is constructed almost exclusively of pheasant-tail fibers, which pulse lifelike in the water. By matching these lifelike artificials to the naturals and by adding a bit more action with a soft-hackle collar, we've built on the success of these designs and have almost always improved our catch rates.

Increasingly, tyers and anglers are also

A two-fly rig and swimming nymphs, slowly drifted along the streambed, enhanced Will Ryan's success on a freezing day in early March.

discovering the qualities that underfeathers can add to nymphs in the form of pulsating, lifelike gills and legs. Philoplumes they're called, or *aftershafts*. Jack Gartside's Sparrow (see Plate 1) emphasizes these qualities by using the willowy, wispy feathers from a pheasant's rump for both the tail of the fly and the collar. It is also tied in the round. For any of the big mayfly nymphs with distinct gills on their abdomens, imitations can be improved by adding a turn or two of philoplumes around the abdomen. Philoplumes, aftershafts, and marabou feathers are also becoming more prevalent in the tying of streamers, as we'll see in Chapter 9.

Swimming Nymph Presentation

The nymph presentation methods covered in Chapter 2 remain valid for these swimming nymphs, with a few additions. We want to take advantage of our fly designs' capability to imitate the motion of the insects. We still need to fish these flies through the water types that the naturals prefer—slow and slack water for burrowers and swimmers, fast water for clingers, and the variety of waters in between these two extremes for crawlers—but we have to be sure they look alive as we fish them.

The upstream and up-and-across-stream presentations are still called for most often, and I'm convinced that the perfect dead-drift presentation is most important only when the subsurface artificial is drifting in the top 6 to 8 inches of water. That's where the nymphs pause, stop struggling, and actually attach to the meniscus. When we're drifting our nymphs on the bottom or trying to imitate nymphs that have joined the

Plate 1

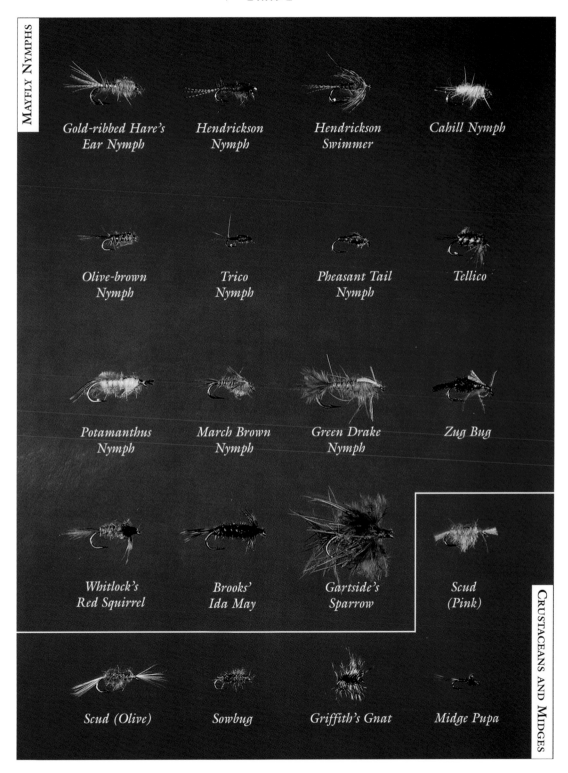

MAYFLY NYMPHS

Gold-ribbed Hare's
Ear Nymph

Hendrickson
Nymph

Hendrickson
Swimmer

Cahill Nymph

Olive-brown
Nymph

Trico
Nymph

Pheasant Tail
Nymph

Tellico

Potamanthus
Nymph

March Brown
Nymph

Green Drake
Nymph

Zug Bug

Whitlock's
Red Squirrel

Brooks'
Ida May

Gartside's
Sparrow

Scud
(Pink)

CRUSTACEANS AND MIDGES

Scud (Olive)

Sowbug

Griffith's Gnat

Midge Pupa

See Chapter 14 for dressings.

Plate 2

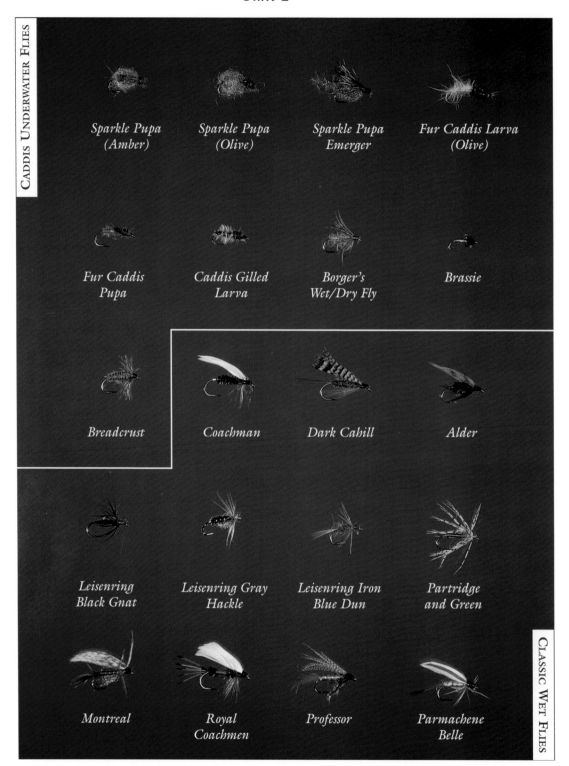

CADDIS UNDERWATER FLIES

*Sparkle Pupa
(Amber)*

*Sparkle Pupa
(Olive)*

*Sparkle Pupa
Emerger*

*Fur Caddis Larva
(Olive)*

*Fur Caddis
Pupa*

*Caddis Gilled
Larva*

*Borger's
Wet/Dry Fly*

Brassie

Breadcrust

Coachman

Dark Cahill

Alder

*Leisenring
Black Gnat*

*Leisenring Gray
Hackle*

*Leisenring Iron
Blue Dun*

*Partridge
and Green*

Montreal

*Royal
Coachmen*

Professor

*Parmachene
Belle*

CLASSIC WET FLIES

See Chapter 14 for dressings.

Plate 3

Gray Ghost *Nine-three* *Black Ghost*

Magog Smelt *Mitchell Creek* *Joe's Smelt*

Muddler Minnow *Cardinelle* *Matuka Sculpin*

Black-nosed Dace *Wooly Worm* *Woolly Bugger*

See Chapter 14 for dressings.

Plate 4

Brooks'
Montana Stone

Brooks'
Yellow Stone

Montana

Whitlock's
Black Stone

Whitlock's
Golden Stone

Albino Stone

Eastern
Yellow Stone

Bitch Creek

Cranefly
Larva

Dobsonfly Larva

Alder Fly Larva

Damselfly
Nymph

Dragonfly
Nymph

Assam Dragon

Ryan's Soft-shell
Crayfish

See Chapter 14 for dressings.

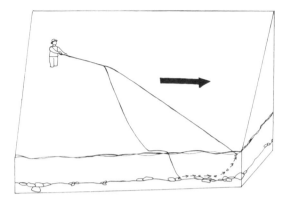

The across-and-downstream slack cast gets the swimming nymphs deep and then gives them lifelike movement as they sweep across the current at the end of the drift.

the flow of water, other than near the surface when they are hatching, do not want to be there. They are creatures of the bottom. Their survival depends on the camouflage of the rubble; their lifestyles are based on it. That's where they hide, eat, and grow. If they've become dislodged and find themselves floating along, they will be making some effort to return to safety. If they aren't strong swimmers, they'll flail away with their legs. If they can swim some, then they'll be moving their abdomens up and down. And if they are strong swimmers, you can bet they'll be moving as fast as they can for cover. So when we are fishing deep, some intentional manipulation of the line to give our flies a little movement will add to their attractiveness. Remember, though, the move-

behavioral drift after sunset, a little animation in the artificial won't hurt. It will, in fact, emphasize the lifelike qualities we've built into the flies.

We can also surmise that any nymphs in

In fast-water flows, since the pure dead-drifting of an artificial nymph is nearly impossible, the lifelike properties of the fly are all the more important.

ment must fit the type of fly we're fishing, in the type of water we're fishing it. In other words, it must be subtle and lifelike.

WATER TYPES

Achieving this subtle movement is the key to successful fishing with any nymphal form. To further our discussion, let's categorize stream flows as fast, medium, slackwater, and still-water.

In fast flows it will be nearly impossible to get a nymph to drift without the water influencing its motion. As we've said before, the fastest water types are best fished with the shortest line possible because the different water speeds and the lanes of current will pull and tug at the leader and line almost as soon as they hit the water. We don't need to add motion to these casts because the flow of the stream is doing it for us. We must try to prevent the various currents from pulling our flies too far along and giving

them unnatural movement. A crawler nymph is not going to scoot across his fast-flow environment in 10-foot bursts of speed. So our goal here is to minimize the horizontal or vertical movement of the fly.

As the water becomes less turbulent and the nymphs more mobile, we do need to add some motion. This is still fairly fast-moving water, and it still exerts influence on our line and leader. But here we can make longer casts and manipulate the fly a bit more. Hand-twist retrieves now come into play.

THE HAND-TWIST RETRIEVE.

The hand-twist retrieve was first described by Ray Bergman in *Trout*, but I suspect it

Across-stream presentations in medium flows allow us to get the nymph deep and to add a bit of motion to it, which is especially effective in cold weather when the fish and the forage are slowed.

had been used by anglers for many years before that. The hand-twist is a repeated rotation of the wrist, retrieving line a hand span at a time. First, with the palm up, the thumb and forefinger grab the line. Then the wrist and hand are rotated, bringing in 4 or 5 inches of line. With the palm now down, the little finger catches the line, and the wrist and hand are rotated back. You end up with an orderly handful of coils that don't tangle. The hand-twist retrieve gives the fly a relatively short, rhythmic movement, imitating the short bursts of many underwater insects and other forage.

With swimming nymphs, we should start giving motion to the fly as it drifts by us straight across stream. If we begin retrieving the fly before it gets to that point, the short little tugs will cause the fly to head straight up toward the surface. And that's not what we want, at least not right now.

As we get into the slow- and slackwater flows of a stream or into still-water lakes and ponds, the combination of minimal influence by the current on our lines and the high motility of the nymphs living here means that we can give our imitations good motion by stripping line back in quick, 1- to 2-foot bursts.

These presentations may not seem very different from the standard nymph presentations discussed earlier, and they aren't. We are trying to get subtle movement of the specific elements we added to our fly to simulate life. If we visualize just what we want to happen to the artificial out on the end of the line, it is easier to translate that idea into appropriate motion through our line manipulation. It is this added motion that causes the new materials on our swimming patterns to move enticingly, bringing them to life.

The author lands a decent fish in early February in Massachusetts, where the trout season never closes. He used a swimming, weighted Hare's Ear Nymph.

Before and During a Hatch

Our swimming nymphs become especially effective just before and during a hatch. The natural nymphs are most active then, shifting about, looking for sites better suited to emergence, or actually beginning the restless rhythm of rising toward the surface and retreating to the bottom. They are now out of their sand, rock, and rubble homes. They are full grown and mature—prime trout food. And they are actively moving about in the water column. The trout feast on them, and our juices should be flowing, too. Whenever we can imitate both the look and the activity of the nymphs, we'll catch more fish.

Our tactics with our swimming nymphs change now, too. Instead of fishing the main drift lines and currents of the streams, we should focus more on the fringes and quieter waters where nymphs will be concentrating. Instead of just giving subtle action to the swimming nymphs as we did when we were free-drifting them, we should be trying to imitate the restlessness that characterizes the approach of the hatch.

On nearly every cast we should be moving the nymph up through the water column and then letting it drift back toward the bottom. As our fly line and artificial drift downstream, we can do this several times. And on the last lift, as the fly sweeps around to directly downstream from us, we need to sweep it up to the surface, as if it had finally made its last rush for the meniscus. To entice visibly feeding fish, we should start this upward sweep just in front of them, à la the Leisenring lift.

The swimming nymphs really proved their worth in my week of experimentation during the Hendrickson hatch on the Battenkill. Even early in the day, six to eight hours before the hatch had begun, the exaggerated movement of the swimming nymph was difficult for the trout to ignore. And as

the hour approached for the big duns to begin appearing, literally impossible.

Swimming nymphs are not a panacea for all our subsurface problems. They have worked for me on several occasions, and I intend to continue using and experimenting with them. Have I abandoned the standard ties and patterns? Certainly not. That would be almost a sacrilege considering their long history and the critical analysis and creative thought behind their development and use. But I will keep swimming nymph hybrids of the standard patterns in my fly vest. And this year I may tie them on first, because I know they've worked for me, rather than as alternatives to the old standbys.

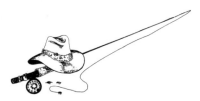

8

STREAMERS AND BUCKTAILS

If there is one universal catchword familiar to anglers of all persuasions, it is Big bait for big fish. In fly-fishing, that "big bait" is streamers and bucktails. These flies unquestionably catch the biggest fish available in any water, and why more fly fishermen don't use them is a mystery. They provide all the challenges of any other form of fly-fishing, including pattern selection and development and a variety of presentation strategies. Yet many anglers would rather be caught with a creel full of suckers than a box full of streamers.

Perhaps this mystery can be explained by the role of tradition in fly-fishing. Cen-turies of artificial-fly development, and the methods of presenting them, have focused on the insects in a stream. There are thousands of them to be studied, and their secrets may never be unraveled entirely. Perhaps the mystery can be explained by the fly fisherman's fascination with imitating delicate, fragile creatures that couldn't possibly be threaded onto hooks and used as live bait. Or perhaps the mystery can be explained by the relatively recent development of streamers as effective flies—only in this century have they come to the attention of fly fishermen worldwide.

This paradox of the fly-fishing community

Big fish, like this Wyoming cutthroat, require big forage and are attracted to big flies, like streamers and bucktails.

may persist, but for those few who do learn how, where, and when to present streamers and bucktails, they will soon become the fly of first choice, instead of last.

The essence of streamers and bucktails is the imitation of small forage fish. As we've seen, once a trout reaches a certain threshold of size by feeding exclusively on insects, it must either find new and larger prey or stop growing. Generally the threshold is around 10 to 12 inches. That is not to say the trout stop taking in insects and switch over to forage fish entirely. They don't. But they must supplement their insect diet with more hearty food items to balance the energy equation and tip it to the side of continued growth. And the larger the trout get, the more they must concentrate on larger prey.

The larger a trout becomes, the more it must depend on larger forage to maintain its size.

Feed Fish

One of the most attractive aspects of feed fish for anglers is that they are available to trout during the entire range of seasons. And unlike many species of insects that live for only a year and attract the focused attention of trout only just before they emerge, forage fish often live for three or four years. They inhabit the same places as trout, rarely becoming entirely unavailable or hidden, and they feed largely on the same elements of the biological drift in a stream.

In addition, forage fish are the primary food sources for trout in a variety of water situations—more attractive because of their size and actions in high, roiled waters, yet still providing a healthy mouthful in the low, clear water of summer. During the prime fishing months of spring and early summer, forage fish, like all other life in the stream, are at the peak of their activity and their vulnerability, so the biggest trout will seek them out.

These larger prey comprise a wide variety of shapes, sizes, and hues. They vary from region to region, from stream to stream, and even from one section of a stream to another. Unfortunately, the study of forage fish by fly fishermen has not been extensive. There are quite a few fly patterns based on common forage fish, most notably the smelt patterns of the Northeast, the Black-nosed Dace of the Catskills, and the sculpin patterns of the West, but by and large streamer selection is often a matter of angler preference rather than trout preference or forage abundance.

As with imitating insects, imitating the particular forage fish the trout are accustomed to seeing and eating can add immeasurably to our success. And as with insect imitation, the first step in doing so is either direct examination of the species to be imitated or reference to some work that has already been done on a particular water. These works do exist, but again, I know of not one book that focuses exclusively on forage fish as they relate to fly-fishing.

Size, shape, and coloration are the particular attributes we need to identify when we are trying to imitate forage fish that are attractive to big trout. Some forage fish are wide and slim, like smelt and alewives. Others are uniformly round, like dace, chubs, or fallfish. And still others have a flattened, bottom-loving shape, like sculpins, small catfish, and young suckers. These fish can be tapered from tip to tip, fairly uniform from front to back, or blunted at the front and tapered toward the back.

The coloration of forage fish generally matches their habitat, and it aids its escape from predation, whether by a combination of speed, agility, and coloration, or through camouflage alone.

Schooling Fish

Slim-bodied fish like smelt, alewives, and shad alevins are schooling fish, often suspended in the water, whether rivers or lakes. Their only protective coloration is dark upper bodies that are difficult to see from above, and white to cream-colored undersides that blend in with the sky when viewed from below. Their primary protection derives from their sheer numbers.

These feed fish are fast swimmers, but do not seek out the protection of cover. Trout, especially in lakes and slow to slack river flows, often attack the whole school, driving it to the surface, where picking off individuals is easier. The schools are often found near their natal feeder streams, both those that drain into bigger streams and those that feed lakes, because they are ascending or descending the stream before or after spawning, because the water temperatures are more suitable than in the larger

Schooling feed fish, like smelt, rely on their sheer numbers for protection, but big trout, like this rainbow that Will Ryan took in a small feeder stream, will chase the smelt up into streams when they spawn.

bodies of water, or because the streams are bringing them a supply of food.

Particularly in tailwaters, where entire schools of these fish can be entrained and run through turbines or bypasses, many are killed or at least become very disorganized or distressed, and big trout and salmon will gorge on the easy pickings. The Vermont state-record brown trout, for instance, was caught in 1991 where the water from a generating station was released back into the reservoir below it. The big brown had taken up residence near that outflow and had gorged for years on dead smelt. It weighed nearly 23 pounds.

Dams, like this one on the Androscoggin River in New Hampshire, concentrate both feed fish and trout because forage moving downstream can become disoriented by the turbines or turmoil of the water, and forage moving upstream is blocked and concentrated. In either case the trout find easy meals.

Variables affecting the size of forage like sculpins, madtoms, and suckers, and of trout, include the size and fertility of the water. Bigger, fertile waters like New Hampshire's Androscoggin River, shown here, produce big forage, salmon, and trout.

AGILE MINNOW-LIKE FORAGE

Feed fish like dace, perch, shiners, and fall-fish use both their agility and their protective coloration to escape marauding trout. They are most often found darting and turning in the shallows and backwaters of streams—where maneuvering would be difficult for big trout—and along the rocky shores and shallows of lakes. They are probably the most difficult forage for trout to feed upon because of these attributes, but when they do leave the confines of their safe havens, which is fairly often, trout will pounce on them.

Included among these agile and colorful feed fish are the young of the trout and salmonids themselves. Big trout are cannibalistic. In certain instances, particularly after an exceptionally productive spawning season, these fingerlings can make up a very high percentage of a big trout's diet. And in streams that see strong runs of salmon, steelheads, or sea-run trout, the resident trout will eagerly gobble up eggs, sac fry, and young-of-the-year for as long as they are available.

BOTTOM FISH

The forage that depends almost solely on camouflage for protection, the bottom-loving sculpins, suckers, and madtoms, have mottled, multicolored backs and sides and wide, flat profiles, and can literally disappear on the bottom of lakes and streams simply by not moving. They are not speedy or agile, so when a trout does detect one, it quickly becomes a meal. Because they are not strong swimmers, they will be found in the slow backwaters of streams or holding in pocket water or the tails of pools.

The sizes of all these feed fish can vary tremendously depending on the size of the water, the fertility of the water, the kind of forage, and the length of its growing season. Of all of these factors, the size of the water is probably our best guide in determining not only the size the forage will attain, but also the size of the trout or salmon we can hope to catch. Bigger fish, both forage and gamefish, will gravitate to bigger water. But at some point the water becomes big enough to satisfy the needs of even the largest fish. What we as anglers need to identify is the most common size of the forage fish in a particular water, so that we can imitate the size the biggest trout in that water are accustomed to taking. In small feeder streams our imitations might be only an inch or two long. In medium flows or in lakes of average size and fertility, the standard patterns are generally tied in the 2- to 3-inch range. But in those rare beauties of streams and lakes where the forage and the fish can grow to impressive sizes, streamers up to 6 inches long, about the maximum size that can be effectively cast with a fly rod, may be our best choice.

Streamer and Bucktail Imitations

For our purposes, streamers and bucktails are defined as any slim, long flies manipulated through the water to imitate something other than insects. The definition has to be this broad because recent developments with a variety of materials, especially marabou and the synthetics, have created a group of flies that are difficult to classify. I call these very modern flies the *soft swimmers*, and they'll be addressed in the next chapter. In this chapter, we'll concentrate on those flies that imitate feed fish and are tied with standard saddle hackles, bucktail, and deer hair.

Gray Ghost

The evolution of the modern streamer began at the turn of the century, primarily in Maine and New York. In Maine, guides and professional fly-tyers at that time began putting long feathers onto hooks to imitate the primary forage fish, smelt. Various stories put the development either in Grand Lake Stream or in the Rangeley region, and the theory and practice was probably coincidental in both areas. At about the same time, a group of anglers and fly-tyers were developing their own set of patterns in New York, mainly from bucktail. Their patterns also endure today and continue to catch fish.

We can safely state, then, that minnow imitations, both streamers and bucktails, are uniquely American contributions to fly-fishing. What emerged from both of these regions were long slim flies that fluttered nervously in the water and attracted big land-locked salmon and trout. They still do.

While the original long-feather flies attracted fish simply by their motion, expert tyers were soon blending colors and materials that not only maintained the attractive motion of the fly, but also imitated the subtle colors of the forage. By blending body materials on the shank of the hook with dyed bucktail, saddle hackles, and other feathers, the full range of the color, shape, size, and motion of the feed fish could be imitated.

In truth, the flies developed in Maine and New York at that time, say from the beginning of the century to roughly the Second World War, are hard to improve upon, and they still form the backbone of any good collection of flies. The Gray Ghost (see Plate 3) remains one of the most popular and productive flies today. The Nine-three, the Black Ghost, the Black-nosed Dace (all on Plate 3), the Edson Tigers, the Ballou Special, and a few others are still effective fish catchers.

Outside the Northeast, an interesting pattern developed by a Minnesota tyer, Don Gapen, in 1930, imitated more accurately the primary forage fish of that region, the sculpin. It was the Muddler Minnow (see Plate 3), and its broad head of flared and clipped deer hair, along with its tapered feather and tinsel body, quite accurately imitated the blunt but tapered body shape of not only sculpins, but also young catfish, young suckers, and the like. It has become universally used and ac-

Attractor streamers can be especially effective in remote areas where trout rarely see anglers or artificials, like the upper Moose River in Maine, shown here.

cepted, and has been modified to imitate a broad variety of forage. It may well be the most popular fly in existence today.

As with other types of flies, particularly dry flies, streamers and bucktails have developed into two general types: *attractors* and *imitators*. Originally they were imitators, their creators having focused exclusively on imitation, as we've discussed. Because the big fish ate the forage fish, imitating those forage fish was the main reason for tying hackles and bucktail onto long-shanked hooks. It still is. But as more and more tyers experimented with different concoctions, a branch of bright, gaudy streamers and bucktails emerged. And at certain times, they outfished the carefully detailed imitators. Included among these attractor flies are the traditional Mickey Finn, the Red and White Bucktail, and Paul Kukonen's Cardinelle (all on Plate 3), but any number of colorful and glitzy flies can be classified as attractors.

As fly-fishing experience has accumulated over the years, the niche occupied by attractor patterns has become more apparent. In the two extremes of the trout world — remote waters where purely wild fish rarely see anglers or lures of any sort, and waters where stocked fish are freshly planted — attractors draw the attention of the fish more effectively than imitators. Also, when streams are high and roiled, as after a downpour, or when runoff has made the cold water opaque, attractors seem to work better. But where fish are experienced and conditions are relatively normal, stick to imitators.

With all our imitator streamers and bucktails, we are trying to imitate the size, color, and shape of the natural feed fish, but we also must bear in mind the action of the feed fish and imitate it in the construction of our flies. Action becomes particularly important with these flies because we are trying to show the trout disoriented or injured individuals.

A healthy, normal-acting forage fish takes full advantage of its habitat, speed, agility, and coloration to avoid being eaten. It is very good at staying hidden or escaping attack. A 4-pound trout zigzagging through the shallows after a 2-inch dace is going to wreak havoc with the energy equation. Therefore, a trout uses stealth, usually after dark, to capture his meal, or homes in on the unusual individual, one that is confused, dazed, or dying.

Wise choices in how and where we present our streamers and bucktails help immeasurably in imitating these vulnerable feed fish, but the action we've built into the fly also must imitate the capabilities of the natural. In other words, much of the secret of successful streamers is the movement in the water of the materials that also imitate the color, shape, and size of the feed fish. Finding the correct combination of all these assets, rather than just focusing on one or two of them, is essential, and that is the essence of streamer development, both historically and in modern times.

With both schooling and agile forage fish, the narrow profiles of the traditional feather and bucktail flies give us our basic shape and action. Particular fly selection is difficult because individual patterns have been adapted to particular forage and even to the particular watersheds where they occur. For instance, the Gray Ghost is considered by many to be the best smelt pattern in the Northeast. But the Black Ghost, the Nine-three, the Magog Smelt (see Plate 3), and the Winnipesaukee Smelt are preferred on certain waters.

The Black-nosed Dace is a good darter minnow pattern where those fish occur, but by altering the color combinations of bucktail at the head of the fly, we can imitate an entire range of colors, from brookie coloration to golden shiner to perch. The Thunder Creek series of flies is much the same. They add an improved shape to the entire fly—the bucktail is tied out over the eye of the hook and then swept back along the shank, giving the artificial a bullet-shaped head. Again, we can imitate a wide range of forage fish with a variety of bucktail color combinations.

And even with the popular bottom-hugging imitations, generally some form of Muddler Minnow, simply by altering the color and type of material with which we construct the tail, body, and particularly the head of spun deer body hair, we can effectively reproduce the range of earthy tones typical of these well-camouflaged bottom dwellers.

In short, there is no list of streamer and bucktail imitations that can be recommended for use nationwide. Suffice it to say, some combination of the three basic fly types, the streamer, the bucktail, and the muddler, is a good starting point; but prowling the local tackle shops, picking the brains of local guides and anglers, and closely observing the local forage will tell you which flies work best in a given area.

Streamer and Bucktail Presentation

There are only two basic principles you must follow to catch big fish with streamers and bucktails. The first is, fish these flies where the biggest fish can find them. And the second is, present them in a lifelike manner. These two principles apply in both moving water and still or slack water, but the specific methods vary some. First, moving water.

MOVING WATER

Many anglers think of streamers as searching flies, but there are better patterns and methods for covering a lengthy section of moving water to locate fish. Streamers should be tied on when you are targeting the largest fish in a stream and when you have a good idea where those big trout reside. Don't be reluctant to try them. The longer you fish any fly on any water type, the more readily you'll recognize the deep holes, the undercut bankings, the heads and tails of pools where food concentrates, and the major interruptions in strong flows that hold the very best trout a stream has to offer. Locating these likely covers eventually becomes almost second nature. So you won't be starting from scratch if you try a different fly or a different type of water; the experience you've already accumulated will support you.

To get your streamer to act like a natural in front of the big trout, a basic store of straightforward casting tactics will help. Within the full 180-degree arc on the stream, from facing and fishing straight downstream to facing and fishing straight upstream, there are only five basic directions in which you can cast: straight upstream, across and upstream, straight across, across and downstream, and straight downstream. The direction you choose is based on what you want the fly to do.

STRAIGHT-UPSTREAM CAST. When casting straight upstream, you want your fly to float down through a good piece of holding water, nearly on the bottom. The upstream water you cast to should not be flowing particularly fast because a fast, hard flow makes it difficult to keep slack out of your line. When you cast directly upstream, either dead-drift the fly back through the good holding water, stripping only enough line to keep close contact with the fly, or give the fly some motion by stripping back a bit faster than the current is flowing.

Straight-upstream casts work especially well with any of the flies that imitate bottom-dwelling sculpins, madtoms, or chubs, which rely on their camouflage for protection. As the imitation slowly floats back down in front of a good trout, either dead-drifted or slowly swimming, it gives the desired impression of vulnerability. And because trout will pounce on these feed fish almost any time they can detect them, this straight-upstream approach works very well. The straight-upstream cast can also work very well for imitating injured or disoriented feed fish, like smelt or alewives, found in tailwaters.

ACROSS-AND-UPSTREAM CAST. The across-and-upstream cast offers more options for presenting your fly to the trout. First of all, it is always useful for getting a fly down deeper because the current is not working against the fly line, and often that is key to finding and hooking deep-holding, trophy-size trout. Because the fly angles away from you and across the current, the trout generally gets a more desir-able side view of the fly, rather than a directly upstream or downstream profile. And because you have better control of the fly, you can use this across-and-upstream presentation in faster flows and heavier, deeper water.

In addition, because of the better control you have of the line, you can do more with the fly. Not only can you dead-drift it or swim it slowly, as you can with the straight-upstream cast, but you can vary the retrieve speed and experiment with the type of fly action that will draw attacks. Often a regular 6-inch strip of line will give the streamer that enticing stop-and-go action. Or stripping in line while raising and lowering the rod tip will give a more consistent swimming action. Or you might find that a fast strip can imitate a panicked feed fish.

Pools are the center of a trout stream's life, and the largest trout are often found in the throat of the pool (left), the body of the pool (middle), or the tail of the pool (right).

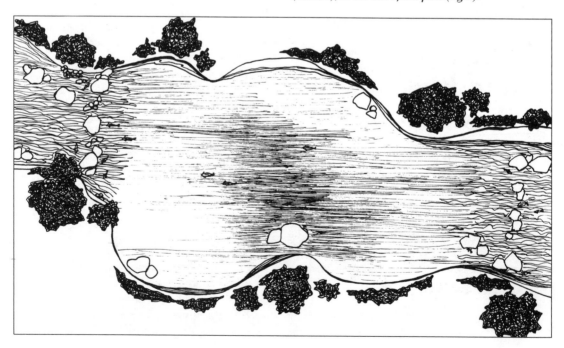

You can also imitate a larger variety of feed fish with the across-and-upstream cast. When the fly is right down on the bottom and then free-drifted or teased back, it imitates the slow, attractive sculpins, madtoms, and chubs, as it did in the straight-upstream presentation. But by controlling the action of the fly at the surface or at mid-depths, we can also imitate many of the agile and speedy feed fish. We can speed the fly along with fast retrieves, we can dart and turn it by manipulating the rod tip, and we can give it that erratic, vulnerable, stop-and-go action that so often triggers immediate attacks.

Also, the across-and-upstream cast imitates what a feed fish usually does when it finds itself out in deep water, where it knows it's vulnerable to predation. That feed fish usually heads downstream and across, trying to get back to the shallows and cover. Rarely will the natural be idly finning out in water it knows to be dangerous, so it won't be facing upstream. Add a downstream, fast retrieve, and trout become immediately attracted.

STRAIGHT-ACROSS-STREAM CAST. The straight-across-stream presentation accomplishes two things that none of the other casts do. First, it covers much more water. By standing in one spot and extending each cast a bit farther, you can explore a long section of stream. On exceptionally big water, the drift of the streamer can also be extended by making a long cast and then, as the fly drifts downstream, playing out more line.

The second is that the across-stream presentation most often uses a floating line and keeps the fly fairly shallow. This is often an advantage when trout are tight in against far bankings or are holding behind stream interruptions or in isolated holes, but it also

The straight-across-stream cast with a streamer covers a good amount of water and gives trout facing upstream a good profile view of the fly.

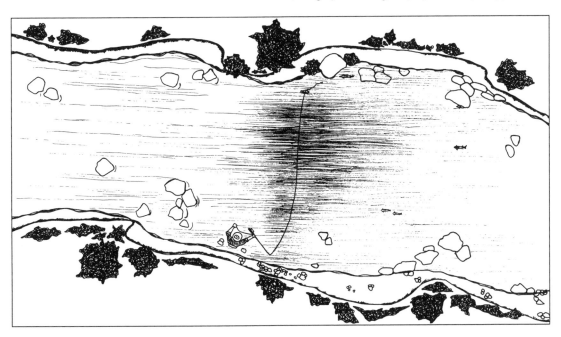

helps imitate feed fish that are in trouble and invariably face their last struggles up high in the water.

The major problem encountered with the across-stream drift is conflicting currents, which can pull the fly away from its intended drift line. This can be combated by mending, but some action in the streamer is not a problem, as it might be with a drifted nymph or dun, because the design of the fly begs action. In fact, manipulation of

the fly during its downstream drift is often required to induce a big trout to take. It brings attention to the fly, and indicates to the trout that it is alive and a potential meal.

This manipulation should be fairly subtle. Again, with the across-stream presentation we're attempting to cover a fairly large section of water, so short strips of line or light flicks of the rod tip will give the fly the desired action without removing it from the desired drift line. And these minor movements also help imitate that most desirable meal, the crippled or dying feed fish.

Presented in a lifelike manner, streamers are especially effective when you are targeting the largest fish in the stream and have an idea where they are holding. Here, the angler uses the across-and-downstream presentation to cast to large trout holding in a pool.

ACROSS-AND-DOWNSTREAM CAST.

The across-and-downstream cast is the classic presentation for the streamer fly, as it is for the wet fly. Yet this presenta-

tion makes some very specific demands and has some very specific goals. With the across-and-downstream drift, the angler must make his most precise presentation. He must swim his fly into a very clear-cut location and make it behave exactly as he wants. But this is the ideal presentation for working a particular trout holding in a particular spot.

Precise presentation is possible because the line that is cast out and downstream is inevitably taut, pulled straight by the downstream current. That means the angler can very precisely measure just where he wants his fly to drift. In addition, by manipulating the belly of the line, the angler can control the speed at which the fly is passing through the target zone, and he can ensure that the fly is giving just the desired profile.

On a recent autumn trip to Maine's Kennebago River for landlocked salmon, I found this down-and-across presentation especially effective. The water level in the river was very low, so the big spawning salmon were all holding at the heads of a few deep pools. I was testing a new three-weight rod and had a small Black Ghost tied on. On an ideal pool about ½ mile downstream from an iron bridge and 3 miles upstream from the mouth of the river, I cast the Black Ghost downstream, but exactly into the far corner of the top of the pool. I swung it very slowly, and about a third of the way across the pool, a 4-pound salmon took. The fight on the little rod was memorable, and the fish was the biggest of the trip.

Speed and profile are considered the most telling details of the success or failure of a streamer, especially in this presentation. They are not difficult to control, if you pay attention to the speed of the current and then alter the angle of your downstream presentation. When the current is slower, increase the angle of the cast by laying the line farther upstream. This will speed up the fly.

The reverse is true too. In faster currents, cast farther downstream, because the flowing water will make the fly swim faster by itself. The speed of the fly is also affected by the size of the belly in the line, and you can adjust that. If the fly is traveling too fast, mend upstream to decrease the belly. If too slow, mend downstream to increase the belly and the speed of the fly.

There are, of course, other manipulations of the fly and the line that you can execute on the downstream drift to attract the attention of trout. Most of them are fairly short, subtle movements that should be made just as the fly enters the target area. One of the most effective is a short strip of the line, or raising the rod tip slightly, to give a darting, lifelike movement to the fly. Another is to put a quick, but limited, bit of slack into the line to let the fly tumble briefly. This imitates a crippled or dying baitfish. And if a trout shows some interest in the fly but doesn't take, or shows no interest in the fly at all, a fast, panicked strip of the fly directly away from the fish can often trigger a fast, slashing attack.

STRAIGHT-DOWNSTREAM CAST. Your objectives with the straight-downstream cast are the same as with the straight-upstream cast. But you would use this presentation only in circumstances that prevent the upstream cast, and for obvious reasons. Because the trout is below and facing you, it will more easily detect your profile and the motion of the cast, so stealth becomes very important. In addition, the cast itself is more difficult. You must almost shock or overpower the cast to put some slack into the line so that it can float relatively drag free when it enters the target zone. A variation of this is to pull back on the rod tip just before the line touches the water. This should give you at least a 10- to 12-foot drift. If you must, use the downstream presentation. If you can, use the upstream.

STILL WATER

In slack- or still-water situations, you are still trying to present the streamer in a lifelike manner in the places where the biggest fish are holding or actively feeding. And locating the fish is the key to success. Blindly casting on a 1,000-acre lake is frustrating and unproductive, so seek out those spots where the trout are likely to be holding (see Chapter 13).

When fishing still or slack waters, you must give the fly all its action. Often this requires medium to fast sinking lines, and you need to experiment with sink rate until you

find the depth at which the fish are holding. Then you can use the variety of retrieves that imitate feed fish.

In certain circumstances, a floating fly line can be an advantage. Particularly early in the season when feed fish in a lake, like smelt, are traveling toward or entering their spawning streams, a fly fished near the surface can be deadly. And if the trout or salmon are cruising near the surface, a streamer dressed with a paste floatant and twitched enticingly on the surface like a dying minnow can often draw hard, slashing attacks from surprisingly large fish. A more extensive discussion of fishing still waters will be found in Chapter 13.

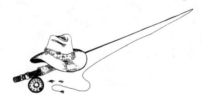

9

THE SOFT SWIMMERS: BUGGERS, MARABOUS, AND OTHERS

A number of modern and productive flies that have gained wide acceptance as effective trout catchers owe their allure to an exaggerated underwater movement, to the unusual use of traditional materials, to the improvement of their action and flash through the use of synthetic materials, or to some combination of all these factors. In many cases these flies fit into classic families, like streamers and nymphs, but in others the flies defy easy labels. What is it exactly that a Wooly Worm imitates? Or a Woolly Bugger? And are they truly streamers, or do they look like nymphs to

trout? It doesn't really matter as long as you have some in your fly box and use them regularly.

If there is one trait common to all these flies, it is their action underwater. They have a flashy, pulsating allure that is almost a caricature of subaquatic life. Where minnows flit and glint, these flies flow and plume and exaggerate the illusion of life. And where underwater insects flail with feeble legs or flex their abdomens to swim, these flies throb and pulse in a blur of motion in the current. For lack of a more descriptive label, we'll just stick with *soft swimmers*.

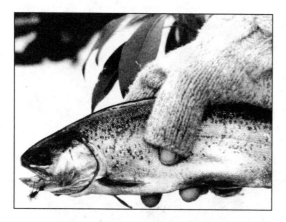

Soft swimmers, like streamers and bucktails, imitate larger forage and attract larger trout, like this good rainbow.

Wooly Worms

Wooly Worms (see Plate 3) started off as fairly straightforward, simple flies. Take a large wet-fly hook, say size 4 or 6, put a red wool tail on it, wind on some earth-tone chenille, palmer a grizzly hackle along its length, and go fishing. The key, to my mind, has always been the palmered hackle, which is usually tied on with the concave side facing forward. It is long and active in the water and must seem fully alive to any prey fish. Because the hackle fibers are longer than normal, they move even when dead-drifted. And because they are usually tied with stiff cock hackle (versus soft hen hackle), they maintain their good action even when swum across a strong current. They are usually tied with weight and can then be bounced along the bottom. But without weight, and with more slender, streamlined bodies, they can be fished across the current just under the surface, where they often provoke hard, slashing attacks. They are workhorse patterns, they're simple and quick to tie, and they imitate a broad variety of food

items, including stoneflies, leeches, and feed fish. And they catch a lot of trout.

As with any successful pattern, variations of the Wooly Worm have emerged. Crystal chenille was developed as a flashy substitute for standard chenille, and its most common application is to Wooly Worms. It incorporates highly reflective Mylar bits, adding a sparkle that attracts attention in many situations, like stained or roiled water. Many tyers are adding extra oversize hackle to the front of the fly as a collar. And the colors of both the standard and the crystal chenille flies have been expanded beyond the black, olive, brown, and yellow earth tones to include fluorescent oranges, greens, purples, and the like. All this experimentation with Wooly Worm hybrids is strong testimony to the effectiveness of the original.

What's the best way to fish a Wooly Worm? Just about any way you can get it into the water: upstream, across and upstream, downstream, dead-drifted, and moved. My own preference, however, is a variation of a downstream dead-drift presentation where I add life to the fly by occasionally stopping its drift with a slight twitch of the rod tip to give the hackle some movement. I also use it as a point fly with a smaller standard nymph as a dropper. The Wooly Worm helps keep the imitative nymph near the bottom and attracts its share of fish, but if they shy away from the big, pulsating Wooly Worm, they'll often pick up the trailing imitator.

Woolly Buggers

Perhaps the most famous variation of the Wooly Worm is the Woolly Bugger (see the accompanying illustration and Plate 3). Instead of the short red wool tail, it uses a plume of marabou fibers as long as the body of the fly itself. This plume generally match-

Woolly Buggers have become extremely popular for one basic reason: they catch an unusually large number of big trout.

es the color of the fly's body, but before it is in the water, the tail seems to overwhelm the rest of the fly. It's when it is wet that the Woolly Bugger's true advantage becomes apparent. The marabou fibers are so soft and flexible that they eliminate the rigid impression a hook shank can give to an artificial fly. They flow in the current and pulse, and are affected by even the most subtle water movement. And when wet, the marabou condenses considerably so that the advantages of the body, especially its palmered, long hackle, reemerge as lifelike. It really is a killer fly.

Because of the marabou tail, the Woolly Bugger should usually be fished as if it were a streamer, using the methods detailed in the last chapter. Of those methods, I prefer the standard down-and-across presenta-tion, where the current does the work and you just follow the progress of the fly with your rod tip. I consider the Woolly Bugger to be a great searching fly, especially when I'm not sure just what kind of forage is available in a river. By using the down-and-across cast in all likely-looking water, you're sure to show an effective pattern to any lurking trout. Woolly Buggers have even outfished my best imitative streamers when I knew exactly what the forage base was.

In Wyoming I hooked some of my biggest trout ever on Wooly Worms. On one excursion I was introduced to Bridger Lake, the most remote body of water in the lower 48 states. My wife, Pat, had convinced me that eight hours of horseback riding and backpacking into the Bridger-Teton Wilderness would be rewarded with exceptional fishing. It was, but only after we'd pitched camp, spent a July night under an unimaginably vivid wilderness sky, and ridden another two and a half hours the next day to Bridger Lake. There the big cutthroats were active on the surface, and after taking a few average trout in the 16-inch range, I decided to try a Woolly Bugger to see if bigger fish were deeper. They were, and I spent an afternoon of astonished pleasure catching and releasing fish that topped out around 24 inches, all taken on slowly stripped-in Woolly Buggers.

On another trip to Wyoming, I was fishing the Shoshone River, that beautiful water that hundreds of thousands of people pass by on their rush to the east entrance to Yellow-

Many of the soft swimmers evolved in the West, where they consistently produce well. Big brawling rivers, like the Shoshone in Wyoming, are ideal places for swimming big attractor-type soft swimmers.

stone National Park. It flows for more than 40 miles from Yellowstone to Cody and rarely sees the crowds that stack up in The Park. In addition, the expanded Buffalo Bill Reservoir provides a fertile still-water home for trout. When they are up in the river, they'll shock even a veteran angler with their impressive size and their aggressive attacks.

My experience was about 10 miles upstream from the reservoir. My brother-in-law, Ron Lofland, has lived in Cody for years and has fished all of the waters within a day's drive of that cowboy town. Whenever I visit, we inevitably start our angling adventures on the Shoshone. In a stretch that was a bit back from the highway, Ron sent me upstream while he fished down. In an attractive bend and cut on the far shore of the

river, I dropped a Woolly Bugger into the head of the pool. Just as it touched the water, a huge swirl gulped it in, felt the hook, and headed downstream for parts unknown. I ran and stumbled and straggled with that fish for nearly a hundred yards, knowing it was big, yet feeling that the 3X tippet I was using should hold it. It didn't. And my brief encounter with a fish that must have weighed 5 pounds and might have weighed 10 left me trembling and determined to tie up more Woolly Buggers.

Woolly Buggers, as well as Wooly Worms, have been adapted and altered as their effectiveness has been appreciated. Mostly these adaptations involve the addition of sparkle and glitter to the body, using the crystal chenille as with Wooly Worms, and the addition of Flashabou Mylar strips or some Krystal Flash to the marabou tails. Again, my experience indicates that the flashier flies are most effective when the water is stained or roiled, while the standard patterns are best when the water is clear. But these flies defy easy parameters, so experiment with them, both in their construction and their presentation, until you find the right combinations of color and action to suit your own home waters.

Marabou Streamers

The marabou feathers that help make the Woolly Bugger so effective have also enhanced the allure of any number of other underwater swimming flies. In many cases, they have entirely replaced the standard feather hackle or bucktail wings on streamers, but often they have been added to standard streamer patterns to give a lifelike action to proven imitations. Other flies have evolved based entirely on marabou, and

they are becoming increasingly accepted as unique patterns, effective in their own right.

Several of the synthetics are also being added to flies or are replacing old materials in flies, particularly streamers. Mylar tinsel is now almost universally used in place of the old metal tinsel. And Mylar tubing is proving especially effective for the bodies of any number of traditional patterns. The tubing, in particular, adds to the realism of the flies because it is woven, giving a good impression of the scales of feed fish; and it comes in a rainbow of colors, from silver, clear, and pearlescent to blue, green, and black, increasing the variety of impressions that tyers can imitate. And because it comes in various diameters, the body shapes of the flies can be manipulated, rather than always tied in the round.

Typical of the old standby patterns that have been improved with both marabou and the synthetics would be the Black Ghost streamer. The standard tie used yellow hackle barbs for the tail, black wool or floss with a silver tinsel rib for the body, yellow hackle barbs for the throat, and white saddle

Ed Lofland strips back a marabou Nine-three at the Bridge Pool on the Battenkill in Vermont.

hackles for the wings. The new version uses yellow marabou plumes for the tail and throat, a black Mylar tube body, and white marabou for the wings. Has the action been improved? You need only look at it underwater and fish with it for a few days to decide.

Another old standby is the Nine-three (see Plate 3), and it too has been tied with entirely different materials. In addition to the silver Mylar tubing for the body and the black and green marabou plumes for the wings, some tyers are adding strips of Mylar Flashabou as a topping or some kinked Krystal Flash to the wings. The Flashabou comes in a wide variety of colors, and a few strips of pearlescent, blue, or deep green add a lifelike translucency to the fly, while the Krystal Flash kinks add sparkle.

MITCHELL CREEK STREAMERS

One of the relatively recent generations of streamer flies to use marabou and synthetics is the Mitchell Creek group of streamers. These flies are an adaptation of the Thunder Creek streamers, which use bucktail tied reverse wing and folded back over the hook shank to form a bullet-shaped head and a slender wing over and under a Mylar tube

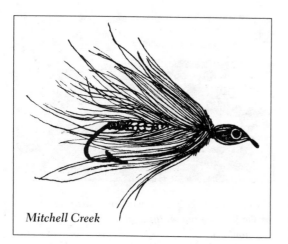

Mitchell Creek

body. The Thunder Creek streamers were developed and honed by Keith Fulsher in the early 1970s and were detailed in his book *Tying and Fishing the Thunder Creek Series.*

The Mitchell Creek streamers were developed by Rod and Dave Mitchell in the Greenville area of Maine in the late 1980s. They use marabou plumes, tied reverse-wing style, instead of bucktail to form the bullet-shaped head and sparse body. Because the Mitchells were most interested in imitating smelt, they settled on gray as an overwing with a white underwing, a similar color scheme to the Gray Ghost's, and added a swath of red thread to tie down the silver Mylar tubing at the back of the fly and for gills at the back of the head (see Plate 3).

Rod Mitchell proved the fly is productive when he fished it in the East Outlet of the Kennebec River near Greenville in 1987. Hoping to attract landlocked salmon that were actively chasing smelt, he was using a 4-pound-test tippet and sweeping the fly across the current. A heavy fish struck, and after a long battle, Rod Mitchell landed a 16-pound togue, a lake trout. It established the world record for the tippet class, beating the second-place fish by 9 pounds.

According to Mitchell, he and his brother experimented briefly with a few other color combinations, but found the gray and white combo to be so effective that they now tie the fly exclusively in those colors, and they have a hard time keeping Dan Legere's Maine Guide Fly Shop stocked.

Will Ryan, who is never happy unless he is tinkering with fly patterns, has added a few embellishments to the Mitchell Creek pattern. He has long maintained that the effectiveness of most standard streamers lies in the color separation of the materials. He points to the continued success of the Nine-three, the Black Ghost, and the Black-nosed Dace as examples. He is also a strong advocate of the lifelike qualities of marabou and the flowing synthetics, like Flashabou and Krystal Flash. His version of the Mitchell Creek blended these qualities with the classic Nine-three pattern. His Mitchell Creek Nine-three uses three colors of marabou, white on the belly, green on the top of the body, and black as an overwing, and he has added streaks of Krystal Flash to the white and some deep blue Flashabou to the overwing.

The Mitchell Creek Black Ghost I've experimented with is nearly the reverse, with black marabou and some purple Flashabou underneath, a sparse swath of yellow in the middle of the fly, and white marabou and Krystal Flash on top. In both flies, the body is Mylar tubing, silver for the Nine-three, black for the Black Ghost.

These three flies, the standard Mitchell Creek and the Mitchell Creek Nine-three and Black Ghost, recently received an extended tryout on the West Branch of the Penobscot River in Maine, where big river-run landlocks feast on smelt almost at will. When the flies were presented in the standard down-and-across-stream drift, they produced well, but the fish they attracted were small by West Branch standards, topping off at only 18 inches.

The thought struck me that the flies weren't getting down to the big fish in the deep runs of the river. The smaller fish, relegated to the upper sections of the water column, were pouncing on the flies whenever they could find them, but the bigger fish just weren't getting a chance to see the flies. To remedy the problem I changed my setup to a sinking line and cast far enough upstream of the deep pools for the flies to get down to the fish. The action of the marabou and the added advantage of the flies scooting downstream just a bit faster than the current proved an irresistible combination. I spent three days hooking, landing, and releasing salmon easily double the size of the fish I'd been catching before, with the big-

ger fish averaging 3 pounds. Mitchell Creeks are new enough that varieties are still being invented to match feed-fish situations throughout the country, but they have proven effective enough to ensure that they will be around for many years to come.

Matukas (Matukus)

Matuka-style streamers are probably best known by American anglers through Dave Whitlock's Matuka Sculpin (see Plate 3), an undeniably productive fly. Its shape and realism are immediately identifiable, with its pectoral fins sticking out from behind its spun-deer-hair head. Less obvious is the terrific action that the saddle hackle feathers give the fly because they are tied matuka style on the top of the hook shank. *Matuka style* means that the section of feathers directly above the hook shank has been stripped of barbules and is tied directly to the shank with the ribbing material of the fly. This method of attaching the saddle hackles allows the tyer to use much longer feathers than he would otherwise be able to, and it gives the fly an exceptional, lifelike movement.

In the standard American method of streamer-tying, the feather wings are attached only at the head of the fly. If they extend much beyond the bend of the hook, they have a tendency to end up under the hook, where they ruin the silhouette of the

A matuka

fly and usually cause it to spin. In addition, streamer flies with wings tied only at the head have a tendency to form a V between the wings and the body when they are not actively moved forward all the time. When they are darted and stopped, as they drift down in the water, the wings separate from the body and the streamer no longer looks like a minnow. All these problems tend to make the trout and salmon turn tail and flee.

Matukas, as explained by Colonel Joseph Bates in *Streamers and Bucktails: The Big Fish Flies*, originated in New Zealand and were actually called *matukus*, a name Colonel Bates championed but to little avail. In the patterns he describes as popular on the New Zealand islands, similarities to some of our most productive saddle-hackle streamers and to our Wooly Worms and Woolly Buggers quickly become apparent. The New Zealand Hope's silvery pattern, for instance, uses a white wool body, silver tinsel rib, blue silk floss lateral line, and honey hackle wings topped with six to eight peacock herls. The color combinations resemble those in the patterns we often use when we encounter black-nosed dace, and the New Zealanders do, indeed, use the pattern to imitate their version of smelt. Another pattern, the Black Prince, has a tail of red wool and a black chenille body ribbed with silver, uses black cock hackle for the matuka wings, and is finished with two turns of black hackle at the eye. It looks like an improvement on a black Woolly Bugger.

We should adopt New Zealand construction methods, though, not because of the popularity there of these flies but because of the increased effectiveness of the flies due to their long hackles and the way they move in the water. And, in fact, many experienced tyers, Dave Whitlock among them, have switched over to matuka-style streamers for almost all their feed-fish imitations.

Recent fly-pattern books usually list only two or three matuka patterns. Inevitably, the Matuka Sculpin is present. And usually there's a fairly generic chenille body, matuka-wing-style pattern. And some recent lists have included generic marabou matuka-style flies. In my opinion, however, even specifically imitative streamers can be improved by using shorter shank hooks, say 3X long to 4X long, and applying the wings matuka style. Specifically, any of the smelt patterns, like the Nine-three, the Supervisor, or even the revered Gray Ghost could be improved with matuka-style wings. And incorporating marabou feathers for the wings, in specific colors and combinations of colors, results in exceptionally effective and active flies.

Here's my pattern for the Nine-three. On a 4X, size 4, hook, wind the shank with black tying thread. Tie in some oval silver tinsel at the bend and some flat silver Mylar at the throat. Wind the Mylar to the bend and back to the front of the fly. Select two black and two deep green marabou feathers about twice as long as the hook shank, and strip the barbs from the bottom section of the quill that will lie against the hook shank, but no more than that. Arrange the feathers, green on the inside and black on the outside, with their curved surfaces facing each other, and attach all four of them to the top of the fly at the head. Put some tension on the tips of the feathers so that the quills lie flat against the hook shank, and wind the oval silver ribbing through the feathers to the eye. About five turns should be plenty. It might help to wet the barbules of the feather where the ribbing is wound through them so that you can separate the barbs and get the ribbing down onto the quill and the shank. If a few barbs do get caught under the rib, pick them out with the dubbing needle. Form a tapered head, whip-finish it, and lacquer. Add eyes if you like. If you've found that it helps to add some colored Mylar strips along the side of your flies, then do so with the matukas.

Matuka flies are that easy to tie, and they have the significant advantage of flowing much more freely than many other types of flies. They can be used in nearly any water, but they are particularly effective in still-water situations, especially when marabou is used, because their added movement is so alluring.

Zonkers

Zonkers have many of the same advantages as matukas and are similarly constructed. The main difference is that the winging material is a strip of rabbit fur, skin and all. The strip is thin, usually about ⅛ inch wide, and is cut from the rabbit pelt *with* the grain of the fur, rather than across it, so that when it is attached to the top of a fly's body, the fur itself flows naturally toward the back of the fly. In the water, this soft, pliable material imparts an excellent swimming movement that fairly exudes life. And it can easily be dyed many different colors, or can be purchased already cut and ready to go in many of the most popular colors.

Like matukas, zonkers originated in the 1930s in New Zealand, where they were called *rabbit flies*. Bates lists the standard pattern as a type of fly rather than a specific dressing and suggests that an endless variety of colors and sizes could evolve from it. And several modern materials have only added to the flies' effectiveness. The major differ-

ences between the originals and the current versions are in the body materials and the way in which the rabbit-fur wing is attached to the bodies.

In the original New Zealand pattern, the body of the fly consisted of some sort of wool or chenille, with the rib holding down the rabbit-fur strip as it does the matuka's feathers. In the zonker version, the body is usually made from a piece of Mylar tubing with the zonker strip tied in at the head and, after the strip is stretched back, at the tail of the fly. Both versions are improved by a beard of soft hen hackle, and you can add tails of hackle barbs, wool, or synthetic yarn. Two other tips help improve the effectiveness of the zonker.

First, build up an underbody before threading the Mylar tube onto the shank of the hook. Because the tubing now comes in a variety of sizes, the underbody can add dramatically to the overall profile of the finished fly. With some lead or aluminum tape, or even some shaped and folded plastic or Mylar tape, depth and breadth can be given to the body. Just slip a larger size of tubing over a deep body and the fly becomes a much better imitation of, say, an alewife. This tip applies to all flies that use Mylar tubing.

Second, when you bring the zonker strip back over the body, use a good waterproof cement along the top of the body to get the leather strongly attached there. This eliminates the gap that can form between the wing and the body of the fly when the zonker strip is wet. The old New Zealand tie eliminated this problem by using the ribbing material along the whole length of the body. Try any number of color combinations, from the natural pale brown of an undyed rabbit with a silver or pearlescent body tube, to the dramatic color separation of a zonker Black Ghost with its white wing and black body.

A zonker

Roofed Patterns

Joe's Smelt

Our last group of soft swimmers are the *roofed patterns*—so called, again, by Colonel Bates. Many anglers will recognize the type of fly by the names of some of the specific patterns: Joe's Smelt (see the accompanying illustration and Plate 3), Jerry's Smelt, Blue Smolt, Flagg's Smelt, Harris Special, and the Wood Special. The feature that distinguishes these flies from others is that the wing feather lies flat against the hook shank rather than on edge. This positioning gives the fly a distinctly narrow profile, yet it maintains an extremely lifelike action because the wing curls down on the sides of the fly just enough to add motion to the entire fly, not just above the body.

The secret to proper and effective construction of the roofed patterns is to get just the right amount of curl from the mallard or pintail flank-feather wing down onto the sides of the fly. If the winging feather just sits on top of the body, the action and appeal of the imitation are lost. To get the proper alignment, measure the feather for length, leaving it just a bit long, then tie it to the top of the head with two loose turns of thread. With the bodkin hanging down below the fly, draw the quill end of the fly past the turns of tying thread until the feather barbs are condensed and lie along the sides of the body. Then tie off a tight head and whip-finish. The effectiveness of these flies can be seen in their motion and color in the water. They look much more alive and fishlike than many of their counterparts.

The soft swimmers do not fly in the face of convention so much as they exaggerate the best qualities of standard flies. Many times this exaggeration is just what is needed to trigger lethargic or wary trout to strike. At other times, the fish will respond as well or better to basic imitative flies. The trick is knowing when to use which fly, or better yet, having both sets of patterns available so that if one isn't producing, the other will. Should you favor one type of fly over any other? Only if you develop a bias. And biases, in fly-fishing as in life, are usually ill-founded.

10
TRADITIONAL WET FLIES

Traditional wet flies have a distinct image in the minds of most fly fishermen. They see flies tied on heavy-wire hooks, with a sometimes complex mix of tail and body materials, and highlighted by wound hackle and rigid quill wings. Yet in truth, even those famous dozen wet flies described by Dame Juliana Berners in 1496 included only four with quill wings. The others used soft hackle, like grouse, partridge, or soft chicken feathers, so they would throb and move underwater. They imitated the appearance and lifelike action of insects underwater, and even in Dame Berners' times, specific patterns were used at specific times of the year to imitate specific insects.

Anyone with even a passing knowledge of the history of fly-fishing knows that wet flies are believed to be somewhat archaic, mildly interesting oddities. Traditional wet flies were essentially the only fly type used from the origins of the sport, which some date to ancient Egypt, until the 19th century, when improved hackle, materials, and hooks allowed anglers to fish dry. And with the advent of dry flies, traditional wet flies became all but lost in the flurry of excitement over exact imitations of floating insects.

When anglers and angling theorists again realized the importance of subsurface feed-

This fine rainbow was taken on a traditional soft-hackled fly with a wisp of a dubbing-fur thorax behind the hackle to imitate a rising caddis pupa.

James Leisenring and Vernon Hidy

In this century, the significance of traditional wet flies in our angling strategies has been highlighted by two men. The first was James Leisenring. While his name is most often identified with a specific presentation method, the Leisenring lift, his more important contribution was in the renewed focus he brought to traditional wet flies. He tied most of his imitations in the manner of the old style, with wound soft hackle, using a variety of land-bird feathers, such as starling, grouse, woodcock, and pheasant. But it was his attention to the bodies, dubbing, and underbodies of his flies that made them so effective and him so well remembered. Leisenring's book, *The Art of Tying the Wet Fly*, was little noticed when it was issued in the frantic years of World War II. Subsequently, however, his friend and student Vernon "Pete" Hidy added more information to the book, and it was reissued in 1971 as *The Art of Tying the Wet Fly and Fishing the Flymph*.

In the reissued book, Hidy expanded on one of Leisenring's classic wet-fly tactics, namely, fishing a wingless wet fly just below the surface to rising trout. On many of his favorite patterns, Leisenring tied his wet-fly hackle over the front one-third of the hook shank and body and used rougher dubbing, with more guard hairs, than on the classic wet flies. This buggier-looking fly, tied without weight and on light-wire hooks, floated along just below the surface, looking much like an emerging insect. Hence the name *flymph*—floating nymph. According to Hidy, it was fished upstream, across, or downstream, and was most successful when the fly was animated, moved a bit, just as it approached a feeding trout.

Both Leisenring and Hidy intended to

ing and the effectiveness of subsurface imitations in catching fish, they transferred what they had learned about the exact imitation of naturally floating insects to imitation of the underwater insect forms upon which fish feed. It didn't take long for realistic nymphs and, eventually, subsurface larvae and pupae imitations to begin mimicking very realistically the subsurface naturals.

As we have pieced together more and more of the natural events that dictate the entire range of the activities of underwater insects and as our understanding of those underwater mysteries has evolved into a body of knowledge, we have begun to appreciate anew the traditional style of the wet fly. Those centuries of use of wet flies, and the thought and care that went into their pattern development, were not mere whimsy. The flies that became staples were based on careful observation of the natural and what it did underwater to attract the attention of trout.

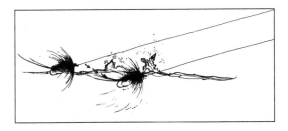

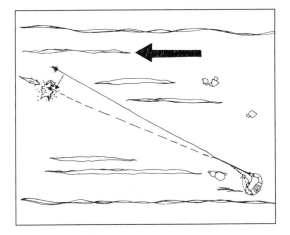

Vernon Hidy's flymph is cast out downstream and across, and just after it alights, the angler gives his line a short, quick tug to get the fly to trap bubbles and float along just under the surface.

put a second book together about the variety of methods that Leisenring had honed over his long and storied fishing career. Both men died before the book was written, and we are the poorer for its absence. The vibrance of the book we do have, however, leads me to surmise that there was too much fishing to be done, too many challenges on the stream to be studied and met, too many hours of pleasure to be gained by marveling at the mysteries of the trout and their world to allow any time for writing that second book.

Sylvester Nemes

The second modern hero of the wet fly is Sylvester Nemes, whose three books, *The Soft-Hackled Fly*, *The Soft-Hackled Fly Addict*, and *Soft-Hackled Fly Imitations*, have almost single-handedly brought the soft-hackled wet fly back into the arsenal of American anglers. The beauty of soft hackles is their simplicity and their effectiveness. Hardly more than a turn or two of soft partridge, grouse, or snipe hackle in front of a silk or floss body, the flies look so sparse that one can barely imagine how well they produce. Many tyers, in fact, wind on a small furry thorax just behind the hackle. Theory has it that this little piece of thorax helps hold the hackle out away from the hook shank during a downstream sweep of the fly, but the effectiveness of the fly without it belies this notion. More likely, the little thorax makes the angler feel better about using these flies, more confident that the fish will take. Either way, with thorax or without, the flies fished in a standard downstream sweep, across the current, or even upstream to rising fish are exceptionally productive.

An American Adaptation

In a uniquely American adaptation of the drab traditional wet flies, color and gaudiness were built into the traditional quill-winged wet flies, especially in the Northeast. Again, this was not simply a flight of fancy on the part of those 19th-century American ruffians. These bright flies became popular because they caught trout, and they often did it much more effectively than the traditional wet flies that imitated actual insects. They became the attractor flies that native

Secluded mountain streams and wild brookies were the genesis of gaudy wet flies. The same flies still work in those situations, like this beautiful but hard-to-get-to stream in New England.

brook trout in New England, New York, and the Upper Midwest hit with abandon, and their primary function was to get noticed.

In the rough-and-tumble streams of these areas of North America, versus the sedate chalk-stream flows of Great Britain, the natural competition for food was, and often still is, the arbiter of which fish survive and grow and which don't. In a flash, the more aggressive brookies were onto the first hint of a meal out in the stream flow. Far from being the easily fooled dolts they are too often made out to be, these aggressive brookies were the very fish that survived and grew large. Were it not for overly ample bag limits and severe degradation of the once sparkling river habitat where these brookies flourished, we might still find that a bright yellow, red, and white Parmachene Belle

(see the illustration on page 123 and Plate 2) was the most popular fly in our vests.

Today there is still a place in our vests for these old attractor wet flies. More and more people now understand the value of pure, cold, sparkling streams; and most of those small northeastern headwater streams that were too small to be efficiently dammed and that flowed in mountains and hills too rough to be cultivated are now preserved and cherished for their semblance of the wild, and for their brookies.

There are also some indications that the value of wild, self-sustaining populations of native trout in pristine streams is being increasingly recognized. Indeed, some fish and wildlife departments are beginning to manage streams to that end. And in many cases the fish that do best in them are brookies,

Where put-and-take fisheries prevail, as here on the lower Deerfield River in Massachusetts, gaudy wet flies often attract the attention of stocked trout unaccustomed to life in the wild.

Wild brook trout were probably the strongest motivation for anglers to develop gaudy wet flies, and no single wet fly has endured with as much popularity as the Royal Coachman.

those competitive flashes of color best caught with those effective flashes of color that are the attractor wet flies.

Ironically, those same gaudy wets are also highly efficient in put-and-take fisheries. When those poor hatchery-raised creatures are dumped into an alien (for them) environment where the food doesn't rain down from above, any bright moving object that might be food is often eagerly taken in by a trout that might not even recognize a plump stonefly as a meal. So although bright wet flies do work well on hatchery trout, let's opt for natural fisheries and wild trout wherever possible.

The two traditional types of wet flies, imitators and attractors, are regaining some of their lost luster and popularity. As both Leisenring and Nemes would point out, in choosing an imitator wet, we still need to

observe and recognize the size, shape, and color of the natural in choosing a wet fly, and we need to have a good idea of what the natural is doing and where it's doing it in the stream before we cast. And we are all growing more conscious of the fact that particular actions of particular insects in a variety of situations are best replicated by imitator wet flies. As we've seen, in particular types of water, competition for food is more important than food-type identification, and there attractor wets are especially effective. But first the imitators.

Traditional Imitator Wet Flies

Traditional imitators are those flies that have the hues, the profile, and the action of the actual insects in the water. They can be winged, or wingless and tied in the round.

QUILL-WING IMITATORS

The winged versions are the stereotypical traditional wet flies, and their usefulness is still controversial. Yet as we saw in the chapter on caddis fly underwater adults and as our forebears discovered in imitating swimming or drowned adult mayflies and stoneflies, winged wet flies deserve a prominent place in our fly boxes. As noted by our forebears, however, winged wet-fly imitations should be used in particular situations, especially to represent a specific insect at a specific phase in its life.

Some of the controversy about winged wet flies comes from the difficulty in getting a properly proportioned quill segment to sit on top of the fly as a wing. If it is canted at all, or the segments don't match well, the fly will not cut through the water in its intended upright position. It will, instead, spin or swim sideways and will not be effective. This means that fly construction, if you tie your own artificials, or the ability to recognize a properly seated set of wings, if you buy your flies, is important. In both instances, we're looking for a properly married set of quill segments that are mirror images of each other. They should be fairly soft, taken from the base of the duck or goose quills rather than the tips, and where they are tied onto the top of the hook shank, the individual barbs of the quill segments should be seated tightly, directly on top of each other. They shouldn't be bunched or curled. The length of the wing should extend to the midpoint of the tail, or if no tail is present, about half a hook gape past the bend.

Quill wings for imitator wet flies are most often selected from waterfowl wing feathers in the color range from white to light gray to black. These wings have three important functions on the artificial. First, they establish the correct profile of the fly. As we noted in the chapter on swimming nymphs, live underwater insects stay up-right. With these distinctive wings, there is no mistaking the top of the fly for the bottom, and the buoyancy of the wings and the weight of the hook point help keep the fly in this upright position. Second, as the fly moves across the current, the wings serve as a keel, keeping the profile upright during the entire drift. And third, wings made from waterfowl feathers are essentially waterproof and will, to a degree, imitate the look of caddis adult wings that is imparted by the tiny air bubbles that adhere to them underwater.

Some of the best winged traditional imitator wet flies have been around for many, many years, and their names have the familiar ring that conjures up visions of old log lodges, smoky bourbon, and big trout.

In my own fly-tying experience, these quill wings are the most difficult aspect of any artificial to get right. If even a bit skewed, they're a hindrance. But in my growing fondness for these traditional ties, I've found that practice and patience pay off. Now I can usually get the wings right on about one in three tries, and when the wings and bodies and hackle do come together correctly, I feel a warm sense of accomplishment that I have indeed created a thing of beauty.

The Coachman (see Plate 2), with its white quill wing, and the Leadwing Coachman, with its slate gray wing, both incorporate the universal appeal of the profile of the wings with the lifelike qualities of peacock-herl bodies and brown-hackle collars. They date back to the 1830s, when a gentleman named Thomas Bosworth first tied them. Their name comes from his profession, coachman to the British monarchy.

The Coachmans imitate quite realistically many of the dark-bodied early caddis and mayflies, especially the little early black or brown caddis and the Quill Gordon, or *Epeorus pleuralis*, which hatches on the streambed and drifts and swims to the surface.

Pat Fuller became a disciple of imitator wet flies when the method began catching big trout, like this one, for her.

The same can be said of the Iron Blue Dun (see Plate 2). Its body of gray to dark gray fur is perfectly complemented by the blue-dun hackle-barb tail and gray duck-quill wing sections. It may be one of the best early-season searching patterns because it looks like so many early-season insects.

Later in the season, old standbys that imitate the lighter-shaded mayflies include the Pale Sulphur Dun with its pale sulphur dubbing and goose-quill wings, the Ginger Quill with its bleached peacock-quill stem body, and the Pale Evening Dun with its pale yellow dubbing and light gray goose-quill wings.

Two other important and productive quill-winged wets often produce well when there's little hatching activity. They are the Black Gnat (see Plate 2), which is especially effective as a searching pattern, and the Cow Dung, which imitates a terrestrial fly often found near meadows and pastures.

OTHER WINGED IMITATORS

Some of our most productive imitative wet flies use other materials for wings. In the Alder wet fly (see Plate 2), the Hare's Ear wet, and the March Brown, mottled turkey quills are used for the wings. And for a whole series of flies, like the Light and Dark Cahill wets (see Dark Cahill on Plate 2), the Light and Dark Hendrickson wets, and the Quill Gordon wet, woodduck or mallard flank-feather barbs are used as wings. Again, careful construction should keep the wings on top of the fly, and they should sweep back at a 45-degree angle to about the middle of the tail. Setting the quill or feather wings correctly is a skill gained with good instruction and practice. Anyone interested in investigating and constructing the wide variety of wet flies that have been developed over the years should refer to Helen Shaw's classic book, *Flies for Fish and Fishermen— The Wet Flies.* She is a master fly-tyer, and she has a thorough understanding of what the flies should be doing underwater and how to achieve those effects.

WINGLESS IMITATORS

Wingless traditional wet flies are easier to tie because they eliminate the tricky quill and feather wings. In fact, they eliminate the wing of the fly altogether. As we saw in Chapter 7, this makes the fly attractive and effective regardless of how it drifts through the current—sideways, backward, or upside down. In addition, the soft hackle that circles the hook adds that crucial lifelike movement to the fly in the water. The hackles often used in these wingless flies also offer detailing to imitate legs, such as the alternating light and dark swatches of partridge- and grouse-feather barbules. In short, the selection of the feather that's used to hackle the wingless wets is all-important; the structure and color of the fly's body and tail are less important.

No other fly patterns illustrate the importance of the hackle feather better than the spider series championed in 1857 by W. C. Stewart, a feisty Scotsman. He enjoyed and used the feathers of a wide variety of birds, but these three spider patterns are the ones that have endured and been cited by 20th-century authors, particularly Leisenring, Atherton, and Nemes. They are the Dun, the Black, and the Red Spider flies, and they are simplicity itself. They use soft blue dun, starling, and reddish brown hackles, respectively, and use only the tying thread and the hackles in their entirety. The Black Spider uses brown tying thread; the other two use yellow. The materials cover only the front half of the hook.

The partridge- and grouse-hackle flies that Sylvester Nemes has recently popularized are as old as fly-fishing. We can easily trace their origins back to Dame Berners and further, if we want to. But it's enough for our purposes to know that they work. I'm never without them.

The three basic flies are the Partridge and Orange, the Partridge and Green (see Plate 2), and the Partridge and Yellow. They're tied with floss bodies that start on the hook shank just above the midpoint between the hook point and the barb. The bodies are very sparse, with only enough floss to cover the shank, and the partridge hackle is well marked and sparse, just a turn or two behind the eye of the hook. A tiny head is formed with the tying thread, and that's it. I've tied these flies both with partridge, which has a gray hue, and with grouse, which is browner, and find they work equally well.

As previously noted, some tyers add a wisp of coarse hare's ear dubbing behind the hackle to hold the hackle out from the hook shank. It does give the fly a buggier look and can't hurt its effectiveness, but it is more appropriate to match the stiffness of the hackle to the strength of the stream flow in which you'll be fishing. Select stiffer barbed feathers for hackles when fishing large swift streams, medium for gentler flows, and very soft hackles for slow flows, for still water, or when you expect to be casting the fly upstream and dead-drifting it.

Although the further refinement of wingless wet flies began far back in history, perhaps no one was more attentive to the details of these flies, particularly the mix of dubbing and how it looked with the tying thread, than James Leisenring. The most detailed descriptions in his list of patterns were of the construction of the body, including the mix of types and colors of the dubbing; the exact color, even brand, of tying silk; and the areas, usually near the tail of the fly, where the undercolor of the tying thread should show through when wet.

In his Blue Dun Hackle, for instance, Leisenring called for mole's fur to be spun on primrose yellow silk with a bit of the yellow showing through. His Iron Blue Wingless changed the color of the tying silk from yellow to claret, and his Iron Blue Nymph, which still called for two turns of hackle at the throat, used the same dark mole's fur dubbing, but called for two or three turns of bare silk at the tail of the fly. Such attention to detail is admirable, especially because Leisenring was striving for exact imitation of what he found on the particular water he was fishing.

Traditional Attractor Wet Flies

Traditional attractor wet flies are those bright concoctions that, at their best, really do approach art forms. They are combinations of color and grace that often wind up in framed

Parmachene Belle

shadow boxes and mounted on den walls. They reflect the imagination and skill of several generations of American fly-tyers whose sense of color, proportion, and attractiveness added an allure beyond utility that caught the eye of as many anglers as fish.

That is not to say that the best of them were more effective people catchers than trout catchers. As we've seen, when competition in a trout stream is more important than selectivity, these attractor flies are more effective than drab imitations. And that situation occurs much more often than most anglers would like to admit.

Most of our medium to large streams with good populations of trout hold abundant forage, but when they become overpopulated, as they can when angling pressure removes the largest fish or when too many hatchery fish are introduced, competition for food becomes keen. In addition, many streams, especially the smaller headwater feeders of larger fertile streams, can be relatively infertile and are largely unfished. Competition in them becomes fierce, and attractor flies work best.

And contrary to popular opinion, in many tailwater fisheries, where the water flows at constant temperatures year-round, forage is often scarce. This is probably because the natural seasonal rhythm of a nor-

mally fertile stream has been interrupted. When its wide variety of water temperatures are eliminated, the wide variety of insects and forage that find a niche at each temperature are eliminated, too. How many strong *Potamanthus* hatches have you ever seen on a tailwater where the water temperature never rises above 52 degrees F? In this situation attractor wet flies are often the best for drawing strikes.

There are literally thousands of attractor wet flies to choose from. J. Edson Leonard lists more than 1,500 individual trout patterns in his 1950 classic, *Flies*, which in 1988 was reissued by Nick Lyons in its entirety and in its original form. There are regional favorites, of course, probably because some flies are more productive than others in certain areas. Or you might adhere to a color theory founded on water clarity or staining, say, yellow and gold flies in tea-stained water, or silver and blue flies in crystal-clear water. But mostly I carry and fish the attractor flies that attracted me.

PERSONAL FAVORITES

My short list reads like this: The Royal Coachman is there because I think it's a true classic, because I think that any fly tied with peacock herl works well, and because it's the first fly I ever tied. I carry Montreals in honor of that city and the nation to our north. I carry the Parmachene Belle because I've always admired the red and white wings and the skill that's required to tie them. I would never be without a Professor because an older gentleman in northern New Hampshire took pity on me in my youth and gave me one, and I caught a 5-pound brookie on it the same day. And I carry a Silver Doctor dressed on a wet-fly hook, not a salmon hook, just because I love the way it looks. I have others, and they come and go in my fly box as my preferences change, or as I lose them to fish and streams or give them away. But you get the idea—pick attractor wet flies that attract you. (See all of the above patterns, except the Silver Doctor, on Plate 2.)

Traditional Wet-Fly Presentation

The traditional method for presenting these traditional wet flies is the down-and-across-stream sweep. While it is a very easy method to learn in its basic form, and in fact may be the best way to introduce an angler to fly-fishing, there are subtle manipulations of the fly line and the fly that can add layers of effectiveness to this basic "chuck and chance it" method.

DOWN-AND-ACROSS-STREAM SWEEP

The basic method calls for casting downstream at an angle that will allow the fly to sweep across the current. Usually the fly is cast out toward the middle of the stream and swims to a position directly downstream from the angler. On small to medium-size streams, an angler standing on one shore can cast to the far shore, and the fly will sweep across the entire stream. On larger waters, only portions of the flow can be covered, but by positioning himself farther out in the current, the angler can cover a broad downstream arc on either side of his position.

On an unusually warm March afternoon, I hiked down to a local stream, the Swift River, just to get winter's woes off my back. I had my little three-weight rod with me, just in case, and a box of wet flies. The stream was low for the time of year. Swirls of trout were showing on the surface in the 44-degree F water, and I hadn't a clue as to what they were feeding on. I tied on a Coachman and swept it through every pool for ¼ mile down-

The classic downstream wet-fly cast is altered by increasing the angle of the cast to increase fly speed, or by decreasing the angle, as Will Ryan shows here, to decrease fly speed.

stream. And in every pool, two or three scrappy holdover trout came anxiously to the fly. I've since discovered that the fish were feeding on little early black stoneflies, but the Coachman worked just fine.

The angle of the downstream cast across the current is generally 45 degrees, but here's where some manipulation of the line can help. The basic action that the angler gives to the fly should reflect the speed with which the natural can cross the current. Too fast, and the fly skitters across the surface and leaves a V wake. Too slow, and the fly swims too close to the bottom, where the natural is unlikely to be and where a wet fly often hangs up on structure. Remember that wet flies mostly imitate active insects anxious to get to the surface or the shore, not deep-drifting nymphs.

Increasing or decreasing the downstream angle of the cast will increase or decrease the speed of the fly in the current. In slower-flowing water, casting the fly farther up-stream, increasing the angle, will get it to swim faster across the slow-moving current. In harder flows, casting farther downstream, decreasing the angle, will get the fly to go more slowly across the fast-moving current.

In all cases, you are trying to get the fly to move at just the right speed to imitate the natural and get the fish to strike. Only when you've had a few trout grab your fly on the sweep will you know just what that speed is. And the speed that is most effective can vary from stream to stream and from pool to pool, so experiment until you've found the ideal speed in each situation.

By manipulating the natural arc that forms in the line between the rod tip and the fly when the line is on the water, you manipulate fly speed. This manipulation is called *mending*. If a large arc, or belly, forms, the fly will probably move too fast, so mend the line upstream to decrease the speed of the fly. Sometimes the fly moves too slowly, so mending a larger downstream belly will speed it up. You can also get a fly to swim a longer distance along a pool seam or undercut banking by throwing in a down-stream mend or two.

The way you move the rod tip or handle the line will also give action to the fly dur-ing the sweep. A light pulsing of the tip gives a darting and stopping effect to the fly, and either lifting the rod tip some and dropping it back, or stripping in some line and then re-leasing it, gives the rise and fall to the fly that mimics an insect searching for the surface.

Many anglers feel that the wet-fly sweep is only a searching presentation, used to cover as much water as possible. And it *is* particularly effective in doing so. Yet varia-tions of the sweep are also effective in cast-ing to particular trout holding in specific spots. The Leisenring lift, detailed in Chap-ter 6, is a modified version of the sweep, as is Sylvester Nemes' slowed downstream sweep with his soft hackles. Pete Hidy also used a type of downstream sweep for getting his flymphs to move just in front of the trout.

All these variations and tactics, and oth-ers too numerous to mention, provide sub-tlety, action, and allure to the fly on the downstream sweep. So when someone refers to it as the "chuck and chance it" method, just smile to yourself—and keep reeling them in.

UPSTREAM, ACROSS STREAM, AND STILL WATER

Traditional wet flies, especially the soft hackles and the wingless patterns, can also be fished upstream, like a dry fly or a free-floated nymph; across stream, using meth-ods similar to those for streamers; and through still water with all the motion added through the retrieve. In short, tradi-tional wet flies offer many alternatives that inventive anglers can take advantage of. And they are regaining prominence with veteran anglers because they work.

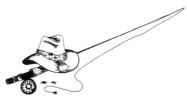

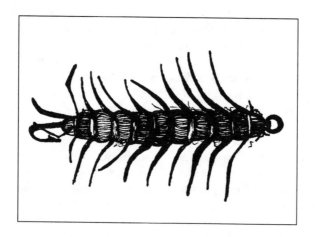

11

OTHER UNDERWATER FOOD AND IMITATIONS

Fertile trout waters are a thick soup of life. And trout, being opportunistic predators, will take in any nourishing life form, especially if it is familiar to them and relatively easy to catch. The more that anglers and entomologists study healthy trout waters, moving and still, the more items of trout food they have identified. On the one hand, that would seem to make life easier for fly fishermen. If you tie on an imitation that represents nearly anything that lives in a particular trout water, then the trout should inhale it as food. On the other hand, knowing that such a variety of food is available can make it maddeningly difficult to match a particular food item if the trout have focused on it and it alone.

As anglers, we can only improve our chances of success by being aware of the variety of food we might encounter in a variety of situations. That, of course, is at the core of our fascination with the sport. Our accumulated experience tells us that much of the time trout will focus on the most widespread and common food items, particularly mayflies, caddis flies, stoneflies, and available feed fish. At other times, however, other forage is more abundant or prevalent. So we should have at least a passing familiarity with other underwater food forms.

Midges

Midges live in astounding numbers in many water types. In sheer numbers they easily rival any other life form in fresh water, but their tiny size makes them significant trout food only in the absence of other, larger prey. But when trout are focused on midges, especially in their pupal form, they can be a significant part of a trout's diet.

The midges' life cycle is egg, larva, pupa, adult, spinner. Only in still waters are the larvae important, and then only at dusk and after dark, when they often wriggle toward the surface, where trout will cruise through them. In both flowing and still water, the pupae are the most vulnerable and available stage. They hang suspended in the meniscus, like mosquito pupae, and their development there and their struggle to emerge attract feeding trout.

One of the most effective patterns for midges is the Griffith's Gnat (see Plate 1), which many anglers feel somehow imi-

The tiny fly sticking up from the far side of this fine rainbow's mouth is a tiny Midge Pupa, the only fly that tempted any fish to strike that day.

tates a cluster of adults on the water. This is improbable (it more likely imitates an emerger) but irrelevant because the fly catches many fish when midges are the main menu item.

Slender pupal patterns fished right in the meniscus are exceptional imitations (see Plate 1). Tie them with short tufts of grizzly hackle barbs at the bend, a tying thread or stripped peacock-quill body, and a peacock- or ostrich-herl head. Best colors are gray, olive, green, and red. The design of the fly helps it float in the meniscus with its herl head right in the surface film and its body suspended straight down.

Because the natural midge is small—rarely imitated on size 16 hooks, more often on sizes 18, 20, 22, and smaller—both the natural and the imitation have trouble breaking through the meniscus, the natural from beneath it and the artificial pupa from above it.

To get a proper look to the artificial, cast up and across stream, but once the fly has settled onto the surface, give it a gentle, short tug. This accomplishes two things. First, it straightens the leader and, especially, the tippet, which is rarely larger than 6X and more often 7X or 8X. Because it is so light, it often lands in a distracting coil or clump, which is enough to warn off a trout that inevitably makes a very close inspection of a Midge Pupa before taking it.

Second, the tug pops the fly down under the surface, where the natural is found. The neutral buoyancy of the fly should keep it close to the surface, or you can add a touch of paste floatant to the leader just above the fly to keep it near or in the surface film.

Because natural midge and mosquito pupae are so similar, the same look and method will work with both. Tie the Mosquito Pupa on larger hooks, say size 16 and 18, and use stripped grizzly hackle quills for the body.

Craneflies, Alder Flies, and Dobsonflies

These three flies are grouped together here because anglers often confuse them, probably because their names are similar. But each is distinctly different from the others, and each of them can be important to anglers, especially when their imitations are fished underwater.

The naturals do have similarities, particularly in their life cycles, which are complete from egg to larva to pupa to adult. And each pupates out of the water, so their larval and adult forms are the main attractions for fly fishermen.

But the similarities end there. They are quite different in size, ranging from the average-size alder fly to the large cranefly to the huge dobsonfly. Their larvae live in different types of water—still water for the cranefly, slow to medium flows for the alder fly, and fast, highly oxygenated water for the dobsonfly. And their life cycles are different—one year for the alder fly, two years for the cranefly, and three years for the dobsonfly. Each should be studied independently of the others to appreciate its importance fully.

CRANEFLIES

Craneflies are those large, two-winged flies that have long legs and slender bodies and look like mosquitoes. Although some anglers effectively imitate the adult with big skater-type dry flies that are skimmed across the surface, imitating the larva is more productive. The larvae are leechlike, sometimes reaching 2 inches in length. They are very good swimmers and prefer still-water lakes and the backwaters of streams. They feed on detritus and vegetation and live in

Cranefly larva

silt burrows, but often move about to new areas and swim toward shore as pupation time approaches.

Imitate them using earth-tone dubbing on long-shanked size 4 to 6 hooks that you've weighted with wire wraps. The overall look is cigar shaped with darker, distinct heads (see Plate 4). They swim in short, rhythmic bursts, so stripping-in line in 1- to 3-inch retrieves works well. Another excellent pattern is Dave Whitlock's Swimming Larva, which uses a tapered piece of tan chamois tied in at the bend of a standard wet-fly hook with mixed brown and gray dubbing for the body on the hook shank.

ALDER FLIES

Alder flies are probably the most recognizable of this group. The adults look like uncoordinated caddis flies and have been imitated for centuries because they sink when they hit the water; thus the venerable Wet Alder Fly pattern has endured. Tie it with a peacock-herl body on a standard size 12 to 14 wet-fly hook with a black soft-hackle throat and mottled turkey-quill wings. Alder flies are active on bright, sunny spring days, breeding and laying eggs and flopping down into the water during the most comfortable parts of the most inspiring days of the year.

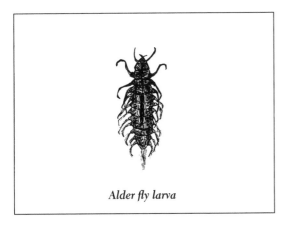

Alder fly larva

Dobsonfly larva

The fish gorge on them where they are numerous, and the alder fly hatch is famous on many streams.

Alder fly larvae are much less imitated, if no less important to the fish. They're tidy 1-inch-long morsels that live down in the quiet wash behind rocks, in oxygen-rich backwaters, and sometimes in burrows in the silt. They do not mix well with predacious insects, like dobsonfly larvae, but where they do occur, they provide welcome feasts for the trout.

Tie them weighted on size 12 to 14, 4X long, hooks with a wisp of light olive fibers for a tail, and a brown to yellowish brown body that's a bit lighter colored on the front one-third of the hook shank (see Plate 4). Add some olive soft hackle on the thorax for legs. Some tyers palmer a short soft hackle up the body for gills, or pick out a little fur from the sides to imitate gills.

DOBSONFLIES

Dobsonfly larvae are the real beasts of the streambed. They are the hellacious hellgrammites, and they are big and mean. They live for up to three years in the hard flows of tumbling streams, and they'll capture and devour any living thing within their grasp, including the nymphs, larvae, and pupae of insects; alevins; and shiners. Their ferocity

is well known to anyone who has naively picked one up and received a sharp bite.

They are welcome forage for trout because of their size, which can reach 3 inches, and their longevity. They take three years to mature, so that even when the biggest of them migrate out of the water to pupate, many younger larvae remain in the streambed. And while they are largely noc-

Hellgrammites love the hard flows of big water, like this stretch of the West Branch of the Penobscot in Maine, where Marcelle Rocheleau (pictured) has taken many big fish.

turnal, enough of them are exposed over the course of the year for trout to relish them and seek them out.

There are several productive patterns that imitate hellgrammites (see Plate 4). Many tyers make them jet black, but a deep brown is more accurate and will take on a distinctly darker tinge when wet. The artificials are tied with short wispy tails, which imitate gills, and with dark brown goose biots at the head, which look like the strong pinchers of the natural. The bodies have either distinct, picked-out dubbing for gills along their sides or palmered hackle trimmed top and bottom. The thorax is a bit larger than the rest of the body, and soft hackles are added to its underside for legs. The imitations are weighted to get them down in the fast water and are worked a bit, rather than dead-drifted, because hellgrammites move well, both forward and backward.

The adults, which are not available to trout, are impressive too, with wings stretching to 4 inches, and with the biting mandibles of the larva still intact in the females. The males have long curved tusklike adaptations that are used only in breeding. The wings of both sexes resemble damselflies in their delicacy, but their bodies are shorter and stouter.

Damselflies and Dragonflies

If the hellgrammites are the terrors of fast-moving water, then the underwater nymphal forms of dragonflies and damselflies are the denizens of the ponds, lakes, and slow backwaters of streams and rivers. They patrol these places in search of any organism they can pursue and capture, and they are very good at what they do. They are extremely mobile, able to both skitter about

Damselfly and dragonfly nymphs are most at home in slow or still waters, but they aren't often found close together.

on agile legs and swim in quick, short bursts. And they have very effective weapons in the form of compound mouths and spearlike tongues, with which they impale individuals from the whole variety of subaquatic life, including all other insects, fish fry and shiners, and even others of their own kind.

Both damsels and dragons follow the same incomplete life cycle, egg to nymph to adult. And both spend the vast majority of this cycle as nymphs. The larger dragonfly, however, generally lives longer, with a two- to four-year cycle, while the damselfly's cycle is usually two years.

The length of these cycles, like those of other multiyear, subaquatic insects, accomplishes two important things for trout and anglers. First, it keeps the nymphs in front of the fish all year. There isn't a single emergence after which the water is depleted of all food-size nymphs. And second, their extended life span, coupled with their voracious nature, allows them to grow to impressive and attractive sizes. As quick and agile as these insects are, their speed doesn't protect

Ralph Ringer took this brook trout when he slow-drifted a dragonfly nymph imitation through the slow waters of the pool behind him.

them from trout, which will eat them whenever the opportunity arises and will actively cruise still-water structure and cover when seeking them out. When an angler finds both trout and these insects in a particular water, he can offer no better imitations than the nymphs of dragonflies and damselflies.

DAMSELFLIES

Of the two, damselflies are the more abundant, but this is offset by the fact that they are smaller by half. They are also much more delicate, in both their nymphal and adult forms. Their bodies are slender and long, and in the nymphal form they have feathery gill filaments at the ends of their abdomens. Imitations emphasize this silhouette and are usually tied on 2X to 3X long hooks (see Plate 4). The nymphs most often take on the colors of their surroundings, so backwaters fringed with deep green algae produce green to olive nymphs, while dark silted waters produce nymphs with a dark

brown tint. Since the naturals have large eyes, add plastic beads or melted-monofilament eyes near the eye of the hook.

One particularly effective pattern is tied in the round, à la Charles Brooks, using grizzly marabou dyed olive for the tail and the thorax area. Another effective pattern is Dave Whitlock's, which he ties as a big hinged Wiggle Nymph.

Because the damsel nymph is agile, both when it walks and when it swims, presentations can vary widely. When the fly is fished near submerged weeds or distinct structure, a hand-twist retrieve that creeps it along the bottom best imitates the stealthy insect that ambushes prey. In open water or at mid-depths, quick short strips of line imitate the strong swimming motion of the nymph.

DRAGONFLIES

Dragonfly nymphs (and adults) are stouter and larger than damselflies, but their populations are less dense, mainly because they have no qualms about cannibalism. The size of the nymph can reach almost 2 inches in length and a third that in width; the nymph has an oval, beefy look. It is a full mouthful for the trout, and because of its two- to four-year life cycle, it is almost always available. Only in the depths of winter, when it burrows down into the silt to hibernate, is it safe, but the trout are largely inactive then, too.

Imitations of dragonfly nymphs range from strictly impressionistic ties, like Charles Brooks' Assam Dragon (see Plate 4), to the less impressionistic Wooly Worms and Woolly Buggers, to the very realistic Whitlock's Dragon Nymphs in olive, brown, and black. The impressionistic ties depend on the lifelike qualities of the materials for their effectiveness. The Assam Dragon, for instance, uses a standard natural brown seal-fur strip wound around the hook shank with only a brown soft grizzly hackle as a collar.

The Wooly Worms and Woolly Buggers are all action and movement. But Whitlock's imitation depends on the motion of a soft grizzly hackle at the back of the head, lifelike furs for the body, and an accurate silhouette to imitate the natural. Each of them will work at certain times.

Dragonfly nymphs exhibit the same range of predation modes as the damselfly nymphs do, namely, ambushing, stalking, and chasing prey. Because of this, the variety of presentations is also wide. Where weed beds, lily pads, and other aquatic weeds can hide the nymph, short, easy strips of line at a variety of depths can be used. With harder rubble and cobble, a slow hand-twist retrieve of the fly right on the bottom is best. And where the nymph might be in either chase mode or escape mode, in mid-depths or open water, a quicker, jerkier retrieve will work. When you can spot cruising fish, especially if the water is not more than 4 feet deep, cast out in front of the fish and let the nymph sink to the bottom. Raise it up through the water column in front of the fish, as in a Leisenring lift, and it will almost always take.

Crayfish

Crayfish is the one food item that rivals big damselfly, dragonfly, and stonefly nymphs in the way it attracts trout. Bass fishermen have been well aware for years of the importance of crayfish in the diet of large- and smallmouth bass (see Will Ryan's book, *Smallmouth Strategies for the Fly Rod*), but trout anglers have largely ignored these important crustaceans. Yet where *they* are available, large numbers of trophy fish are often available because crayfish are usually numerous and certainly nutritious.

It is important to note, however, that certain times of the year and probably cer-

Crayfish

tain sizes of crayfish are more important than others. Crayfish are active in a much narrower range of water temperatures than trout. Generally their optimum temperatures are above 65 degrees F, so in trout waters they are most active in the summer months. In addition, trout prefer soft-shelled crayfish just after they have molted, and one- and two-year-old crayfish molt most often, about 10 times per year. These one- and two-year-olds generally range from ¾ inch to 1¼ inches in length. Smaller than that, the crayfish are difficult for trout to catch; larger, they molt rarely and stay hard-shelled. One final fact is that the colors of crayfish mimic their surroundings, and soft-shelled crayfish are lighter colored until their shells harden.

With this information, we can develop a pattern strategy to use soft materials, not hard or epoxied materials; keep the length of the entire fly under 1¼ inches; and use materials that are a shade lighter than the habitat of the crayfish.

The pattern Will Ryan has developed incorporates all these elements (see the accompanying illustration and Plate 4). On a

2X long, size 4 to 8, hook use a mix of rabbit fur and Antron dubbing for the body. For the carapace, tie in a clump of bucktail at the bend. Fold it back over the hook to form the shell, the thorax cover, and the tail. Note that the tail of this pattern is at the eye of the hook. The claws of the pattern are made of fox-fur fibers; they are tied in about midway along the shank and extend back only to the bend of the hook. Pick out some underfur to imitate gills. The fly can be tied un-weighted, or upside down with weight along the shank that will keep the hook point up.

Fish the pattern anywhere that trout will find crayfish, still water or flowing, but bear in mind that stream or lake bottoms consisting of larger rocks and cobble provide excellent cover and hiding spots for crayfish. Seek out the gravel bottoms below these areas in streams or the sandy shoals adjacent to them in lakes. Fish right on the bottom and very slowly, moving the fly with a hand-twist retrieve. (See details of the hand-twist retrieve in Chapter 7.)

Crayfish imitations can bring rousing strikes from the largest fish in a lake or stream, as Will Ryan, shown here on the West Branch of the Ausable in New York, has proved many times.

Scuds and Sowbugs

While crayfish are the big-food-item crustacean, it is the scuds and sowbugs that provide trout with a constant supply of food. They demand the same quality of water that trout do—pure, cold, and well oxygenated—but they absolutely thrive in slightly alkaline waters, rich in the minerals necessary for shell regeneration. Scuds and sowbugs, like other crustaceans, shed their shells at regular intervals.

They are not large food items, rarely reaching 1 inch in length, but where conditions are optimal, scuds and sowbugs occur in huge numbers. And even where conditions are not ideal, they are important components of a trout's diet. Anglers in the West are mindful of the importance of scuds and sowbugs, but anglers throughout the continent gauge a trout's wildness by the pink to

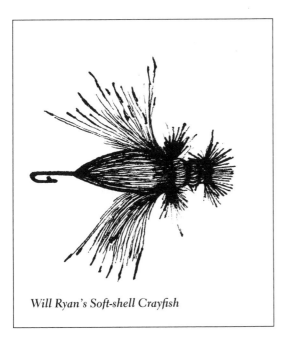

Will Ryan's Soft-shell Crayfish

Scuds in the flow and sowbugs clinging.

orange tint of its flesh, and that tint comes from crustaceans, usually scuds and sowbugs.

SCUDS

Although similar in their size and water-quality demands, scuds and sowbugs are quite different in their look and in the way their imitations are fished. Scuds are shrimp-like and often referred to as *freshwater shrimps*. Their colors range from olive gray to dark gray. But trout especially relish soft-shelled scuds, as they do soft-shelled crayfish, and when scuds are newly molted, they take on a distinctly lighter color, a tannish pink, which helps explain the popularity of that color in imitations. Like all other crustaceans, they turn bright pink to red only when they are dead, a function of the carotene in their shells. And it is this carotene that makes trout flesh pink to orange.

In tying scud patterns it is important to recognize that scuds swim exceptionally well, and when they are swimming they are straight-bodied. Only when they are in danger, or out of water in your hand, or dead, do they take on that rounded, shrimplike curl. Tie scud patterns on weighted, straight-shanked hooks, using a coarse dubbing (see Plate 1). Tie an overbody cut from cellophane or clear plastic, and rib it with brass or copper wire. The natural has many segments, 13 in fact, so the ribbing should be distinct and closely spaced. All crustaceans have four antennae, so add some barred flank-feather barbs at the head if you like. But bear in mind that scuds swim equally well forward and backward, so this detail can be distracting. Pick out some of the dubbing under the body to imitate legs and gills.

Because scuds do swim well and occur in most trout waters, they can be fished in almost any type of water—moving or still—and at almost any location in the water—bottom, mid-depth, or shallow. They use cover and underwater vegetation well, so present scud patterns to the trout near underwater

Scuds and sowbugs are found in a wide variety of waters, including the Madison River in Yellowstone National Park, pictured here, where Ron Lofland plies the waters.

weed beds, along weed lines, and in and around structure. In still water, let them sink some and retrieve them with a variety of speeds and strip lengths. Fish them in mid-depths and along the bottom, but stay in fairly shallow water, say up to 4 feet, because scuds are vulnerable, and rare in deeper waters.

In flowing water, scuds just float along with the current, both accidentally and intentionally as they disperse, but they can also scoot across current, and up and down in the water column. An ideal presentation would include dead-drifting the fly for most of the cast, but giving it an occasional twitch, and then letting it swing across the current and up through the water at the end. Trout feed on so many scuds, and often so casually, that a strike indicator will help detect the gentle take.

SOWBUGS

Sowbugs have an entirely different look than scuds. They are flat little creatures with distinct legs sticking out from the sides of their segmented bodies. They can't swim at all, but rather crawl along and through vegetation. A favored plant is watercress; hence they're often called *cress bugs*. They're about the same size as scuds, ranging up to an inch in length; and they're earth toned, generally dark gray to brown.

Tie their imitations by simply dubbing a coarse mix of fur onto a weighted hook (see Plate 1). Trim the dubbing top and bottom to give the fly a flat look, with legs sticking out the sides. Some tyers add a shell back, from cellophane or Swiss straw, and rib the body with wire, but this is optional.

Sowbugs are difficult to fish in still water because they don't swim and because trout feed on them as if they were picking fruit from a tree. You might draw a strike if you free-drift an imitation down through the water in front of a cruising trout, but you'll have much greater success dead-drifting the imitation in flowing water, especially just below vegetation beds. Again, the take will be subtle, so a strike indicator will help.

Leeches, Lampreys, Snakes, and Amphibians

There is a whole array of long, skinny, bottom-loving creatures that trout will eat if given the chance. They live in both still and moving waters, and they are important, if for no other reason, because the trout that take them are usually large and usually take them at every opportunity. These creatures are the stuff of nightmares, or if you land an 8-pound rainbow on an imitation of one, the stuff of sweet dreams. They're the leeches, snakes, lamprey eels, tadpoles, salamanders, and other such smooth-skinned, elongated creatures.

They may explain the popularity and productivity of some of the generic artificials that always catch fish, flies like the Woolly Bugger, the Wooly Worm, the Zonker, the Muddler in a number of its variations, and the wet flies like the Sparrow and the Casual Dress. Other less well known patterns have been developed, especially by Dave Whitlock, to imitate particular creatures, but whether you opt for impressionistic or realistic patterns, you should follow two or three principles when tying on and fishing these flies.

First of all, most of these creatures take on the colors of the water and/or the bottom of the lake or stream. Dark, silty waters produce dark, earthy creatures; clear rocky water, lighter, more silvery creatures. Black is always productive because leeches, perhaps the most prevalent and widespread of these animals, are usually very dark brown to black themselves.

Second, these creatures live on or near the bottom, so they should be fished there, especially in lakes or ponds, but also in the slow or slack water of streams and rivers. And third, they are generally good swimmers, so you should make your fly swim too, in a steady, if not fast, retrieve. These flies can be extremely productive in still water, but most of these animals occur in moving water too, so don't ignore their potential in streams and rivers where big fish live. Just remember to keep them deep and keep them moving.

Drowned Terrestrials

Look through nearly any fly-pattern book, and when you come to the terrestrial section, you'll find plenty of patterns for ants,

hoppers, crickets, beetles, inchworms, leafhoppers, bees, and caterpillars, all tied on dry-fly hooks. Yet if you spend some time watching terrestrials on moving or still water, you are likely to notice that many of these land-born insects are not designed to float or swim on water. In fact, given a little motion to the stream or wind on the lake, you'll see that these insects quickly become submerged, where trout are much more likely to feed on them. After all, without the distortion of looking up through the meniscus and into the sky, the trout have a much better view of terrestrials, and will quickly inhale them.

Terrestrials, especially ants and beetles, are available to fish throughout the year, and when trout are not focused on some specific or impending emergence, they can be caught with terrestrial imitations. The key is to fish them where the trout are taking naturals. If the fish have no reason to feed on the surface, which is often the case when there is no hatch, then fish a terrestrial pattern deep, where the fish are holding. Deep-drifted Wooly Worms, in addition to their many other commendable traits, make excellent drowned-caterpillar imitations. Fishing deep is the strategy we use for any other insect in the water, so we shouldn't doggedly fish terrestrials on the surface when no fish are showing.

Fishing terrestrials wet is quite the same thing as fishing nonswimming nymphs wet. They should be dead-drifted through a good feeding lane or right down in front of a fish in view. Because terrestrials are land born, any place with bushes, logs, and branches overhanging the water provides potential feeding sites. And because both terrestrials and trout favor shade rather than direct sunlight, fish the shaded shore of the stream, especially in the morning and afternoon.

While I've generally just drowned my dry-fly versions of terrestrials to fish them wet, more and more now I'm tying them on wet-fly hooks, because more and more I'm fishing them down in the water.

Eggs

With the proliferation of pickled salmon eggs on the bait market, it would seem that imitation fish-egg flies would be logical choices nearly any time you go out. And this isn't a bad idea when you are angling for freshly stocked hatchery trout. When it is dropped into the water from above and drifts along the bottom, an egg fly looks and acts not like something in nature but like the food a stocked trout is used to.

In the natural scheme of things, however, there are specific times when egg flies imitate an item on which wild trout feed with relish: During and just after trout and salmon spawn, and in rivers where suckers spawn, eggs that are not adequately protected in nests, or redds, will wash down the streambed and quickly be eaten. In streams that suffer a sudden spate of water during or just after the spawn, many of the newly laid eggs will be washed away, too, and waiting trout will gobble them up like . . . well, caviar.

Brook trout, browns, and other char are fall spawners. They'll find appropriate rocky and gravelly runs that receive a regular flow of cold, well-oxygenated water, make two or three redds, and lay and fertilize their eggs.

Cutthroats, rainbows, steelhead, and suckers spawn in the spring, often running up into rivers and feeder streams very early in the year to spawn. Pacific salmon spawn at various times, from June right into winter. In short, in most areas of the continent, fishing with egg flies can be very productive at some point during the year.

Yarn for tying egg flies is available from most fly-tying supply houses and comes in a variety of fluorescent colors; pink, orange, and chartreuse are favorites. Many tyers add a dot of contrasting color to represent the eye or developing embryo in the egg.

Egg flies are free-drifted right on the streambed with no drag whatsoever. They are effective whenever real eggs are available, but especially in turbid water because their bright colors signify food to hungry trout. The pickups are very subtle, especially in the cold water of late winter, but the result of that barely noticeable take can be a huge steelhead blasting out of the water.

This listing of other trout foods is far from exhaustive. There are hundreds of other organisms in both still and moving water that can be successfully imitated to catch trout. The few listed in this chapter are important and fairly universal throughout North America, but never ignore local foods, fly patterns, or tactics. Much experience and experimenting have gone into some of these seemingly wildcat patterns, and they may just be the best fly for a particular water at a particular time. Fly-fishing has evolved to its present state because of this kind of experimentation. And fly fishers, I hope, will continue to delve into the mysteries of what trout eat, when they eat it, and how it can be effectively imitated.

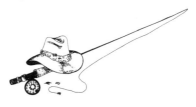

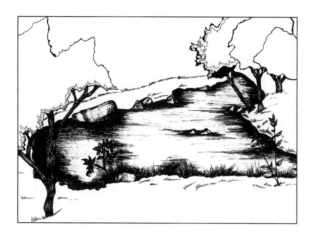

12

READING AND FISHING FLOWING WATER

All that we've discovered, in this book and hundreds of others, about the biology of trout, what they feed on, and how to imitate their forage forms the basis of our fascination with fly-fishing. Each bit of information about underwater life is unique and interesting in itself, and as we accumulate more of these bits, a picture of the complexity of aquatic interactions begins to come into focus. Sometimes the focus is sharp, as when a trout is rising to an emerging Hendrickson Nymph. At other times, the focus is blurred, as when a multiple hatch confounds our logic.

It is when we get to the river, when we actually set foot into fertile, flowing water, that we see how all these bits of information blend into a flowing alien world, beautiful and mysterious, and more than worthy of our curiosity and our appreciation. We are sometimes slow to realize that the medium of this world—the moving water itself—is what unifies it and makes it unique.

As we enter the stream, the flow of the water transforms us from mere students of its various parts to participants in its dramas, and we quickly learn to study the medium, too, to study the way the water flows and how its inhabitants react to its everchanging moods.

Even though the process of hatch matching, bug identification, and precision fly-tying can be quantified, it is much more difficult to lay out specific rules about the way that brooks, streams, and rivers flow and affect all the creatures that live in them. Certainly we can talk about the hydraulics of streams, about curving pools, about seams in the water, and about pocket and riffle water; and we will. But the infinite variety of flowing water accounts for much of our interest in fly-fishing. From tiny mountain brooks to fertile, meandering streams to mighty, thunderous rivers—they're all unique. Even flows with similar characteristics, such as gradient, volume, and fertility, individually exhibit their own character, harbor their own secrets, and provide their own delights.

What follows in this chapter, then, is far from exhaustive. It is only a thumbnail sketch of what to look for in a trout stream, providing, in a rudimentary way, a baseline of information from which to approach any of the streams you might encounter. Only a continuously inquisitive nature will allow

Flowing water keeps us fascinated because of its infinite variety and the countless ways trout exploit it.

anglers to fully enjoy the flowing waters of their own world and to build upon past experience to develop new appreciation for the many unknowns about flowing water and the creatures that live in it.

Species Preferences

In attempting to locate trout in flowing waters, it is important to know the particular species of fish that inhabit a stream, whether browns, brookies, cutthroats, or rainbows. While they all need pure, fertile water in which to thrive, each has specific preferences for water types and inhabits certain areas of the stream more frequently than the others. For instance, if we concentrate our efforts on the strong flows at the base of rapids where rainbows and cutthroats are likely to be found, and the stream supports a higher percentage of browns, then our success at locating fish will be diminished. Browns much prefer slower flows, approaching slack water. Certainly we might catch a brown or two in faster waters, but concentrations of the best browns will be in a different type of water from where we would find most rainbows.

BROWNS

Brown trout, especially during bright daylight, seek out safe, comfortable water, where they can rest easily and conserve their energy without fear of attack from the skies or the waters. Their water-temperature tolerance is higher than other trouts', but their optimal water temperatures are similar to brookies' and rainbows', with 55 to 65 degrees F the best for active feeding and growth. Browns are found more often in the slower tails of pools, under bankings, below snags, and behind other river structure. And

Different species of fish prefer different types of water.

Brown trout lurk in the slow deep water of a stream. They embrace the security of the structure of the banks and depths, emerging at dusk and after dark to feed and forage.

the biggest of them cruise these slower waters at dusk and after dark, actively seeking big forage.

BROOK TROUT

Brookies are the middle-class fish. They have a lower tolerance for warm water, but they can thrive in much less fertile water than other species and have a higher tolerance for acidic waters; hence they are often found in high mountain feeders and streams. They are therefore much more opportunistic feeders than most other species and will attack almost any piece of forage, or artificial fly, that floats by. They're found in many other water types, too, but fill the niche between the slower waters browns prefer and the faster waters of the rainbows and cutthroats.

Brookies can survive in a wide variety of waters, but are found most often nowadays in cold, relatively infertile mountain streams.

species. When they are displaced, they'll seek out the waters where the other fish aren't, so if you've got both rainbows and cutthroats in a particular river, the cutthroats will avoid the rainbows and be found in the less turbulent waters.

A prime example of this is Yellowstone National Park's idyllic Slough Creek. It has become something of a tradition for Pat and me every time we're in the West to travel to Slough Creek with Ron Lofland and his wife, Yvonne, for a day of fishing and a sumptuous picnic. Slough is inhabited by native cutthroats and by rainbows, which were introduced many years ago, and we can almost predict which fish to expect where. The separation of the two species is not total, however, as we also catch a fair number of hybrids, known locally as *cutbows*.

RAINBOW TROUT

Rainbows have the same comfort range of water temperatures as other trout, namely 55 to 65 degrees F, but much prefer more highly oxygenated, swifter-flowing water. Many anglers bypass this type of water because of its strong, hard current without realizing that the trout have combined their water preference with the rigors of the energy equation by taking refuge in the numerous small pockets of slow water behind bottom rocks and boulders. Fast water over big rocks is the best place to find rainbows.

CUTTHROATS

Cutthroat trout have much the same preferences as rainbows and, where they are isolated from other species, will seek out fast, highly oxygenated water. Cutthroats, however, are much less tolerant of other species of trout, such as the rainbows that are too often introduced into their waters, and are easily displaced by the more aggressive

Rainbows and cutthroats are fast-water lovers, but they are not usually found together since cutthroats are easily displaced by rainbows.

The Basics of Survival

In all cases, trout must concern themselves with the three basics of survival: food, safety, and spawning. First, the food they eat must offset the energy they expend to catch it— the energy equation. Otherwise, they'll soon outstrip their energy reserves and die. The distance between holding and resting water and optimal feeding water is a critical factor in the energy equation.

A trout can't seek out the best shelter in a stream only to find that the best feeding area is 200 yards upstream. Holding water needs to be close to a good feeding station, and trout compromise between the two. They will, in other words, find a spot nearest

The basics of trout survival are food, shelter, and good spawning gravel, all in fairly close proximity.

the best concentrations of food in which to rest safely. A flow of water that pushes food items together, making it easier for the trout to ingest a large number of food bits, is a primary spot for active, feeding fish.

Second, to escape the predation of birds, otters, and bigger fish, trout need the protection of deep water, or overhead protection, or a complex of snags and deadfalls, or some combination of all these features. They need access to a spot in the river where they are relatively secure yet close enough to their feeding sites that they won't die in the effort to find food.

To these fundamental needs for concentrations of food and safe havens can be added another. Trout, like all animals in the wild, lead basic lives: survive, grow, and reproduce. While spawning itself is not a key to actually angling for trout, because it occurs for a relatively brief time and because only the most shortsighted angler would interrupt the process that keeps fish in his river, it is important for the angler to recog-

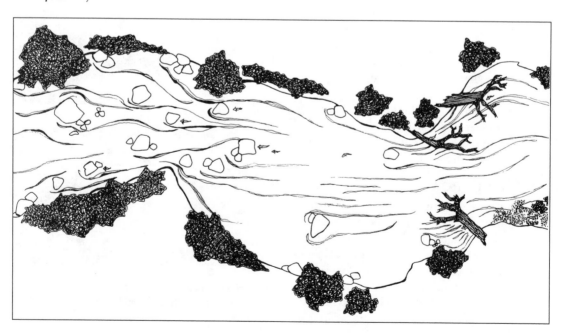

nize that good spawning sites will be fairly close to the areas that meet the trout's needs for food and shelter, the areas where the trout spend most of their lives. Nonmigrating fish cannot travel great distances to find appropriate spawning gravel, as anadromous trout and salmon do.

Thus if you've got a stream that flows over smooth bedrock for a mile and a half, then follows a streambed of gravel and sand for 300 yards, and then rushes for another half mile over hard rubble, trout will usually be found in their highest concentrations near the good spawning gravel. When, as is often the case, these ideal spawning areas are sprinkled all along the length of a stream, they do not isolate the best trout areas. But on quite a few flows, the best spawning sections pinpoint the best angling areas.

Pools

The primary place to seek trout in flowing water is in pools. And any angler who's ever been asked for advice would be remiss if he didn't start by telling you to fish the best pools first. Pools are where the essential elements of a trout stream come together in a relatively short segment of the stream, and they generally include all the characteristics that attract trout—protective holding water, good feeding spots, and usually some good spawning gravel nearby.

Pools, however, come in a huge variety of shapes and sizes. Among many other possibilities, they can be S-shaped or hourglass-shaped, right-angle or top-bulging. They can have hairpin turns or sweeping turns. They can be hundreds of yards long or only a good fly cast from head to tail. But they are all recognizable because they all have certain standard characteristics.

Some descriptions of pools focus only on the slow, deep, flat water of the deepest

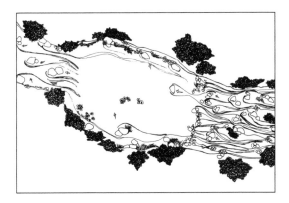

Pools come in myriad shapes and sizes, but they all contain a throat, body, and tail.

section. But no pool will be without these important features: a head, or throat, where the water narrows and enters; a body, or flat, where the water deepens and the current slows; and a tail, where the waters become shallow, gather speed, and then spill over into the next stream feature.

The Head, or Throat

The head, or throat, of the pool is where I'm always drawn first. The water gathers and flows over some impediment in the stream that narrows it and then dumps its full force into deeper water. In the extreme case, the throat can be a waterfall.

Most throats of pools are good places for feeding fish to lie because they generally come at the end of a riffle or series of rapids where many insects and crustaceans develop. Because of the way the throat concentrates the flow of water, the food is concentrated, too, and the fish are nearby.

Throats can be fairly short, like waterfall throats, with the water suddenly dropping into the pool, but more often throats are gradual, slowly constricting and concentrating at the head of the pool. Sometimes the throat can even be longer than the flat of the pool, but it remains a prime angling spot because it contains food and the safety of the pool proper is nearby.

Throats not only hold the most food and the best trout, they are the easiest to fish. All three of these facts help explain my affinity for the throats of pools. The contrary currents from the upstream side are fairly well eliminated by the narrowing of the throat. The water upstream from the throat is also inevitably shallower, with fewer holding sites, making it difficult for fish to find comfortable water. And the water in the throat of the pool is easy to read. The seams in a throat, where slower water meets faster water, are well defined and attractive to trout that want to ambush prey from the slower water.

THE BODY, OR FLAT

The slack, flat waters of pools can be difficult and frustrating to fish. First of all, they're often very deep, with the dark waters used by the fish only as resting sites. Second, slack water is often relatively featureless, with few if any instream logs or rocks around or beneath which fish can feel secure. And third, in the very competitive world of trout, the fish that get to the forage first, at the head of the pool, are usually the bigger ones. This means that the fish holding in the depths of the pool are rarely feeding, and the feeding fish in the body of the pool are probably the smallest fish available.

Should you ignore the flats altogether? Not necessarily, especially if you have evidence of active feeding or if the pool is relatively small with a poorly defined throat, body, and tail. But you should not automatically rush to the flat. Only after you've thoroughly plied the better waters at the head and tail of the pool should you spend time on the body.

THE TAIL

The tail of the pool is attractive to the biggest trout because it is a prime forage area. Insects that develop in the pool wash down into the tail, and the forage fish that come up into the pool from downstream are most vulnerable to attack. The tail usually holds the best fish but is also the most difficult area for the angler to approach and fish successfully. The water at the tail is likely to hold varying currents, making presentations difficult. And because the water has gotten shallower toward the tail and usually has few features, the fish are extremely wary, making careful approach essential and precise presentation important.

Pools aren't always as straightforward as this discussion of their basic characteristics might imply. They take many shapes and sizes, bend around corners, or cut back against opposing banks. They can often hide their most attractive features.

CURVING POOLS

The curving pool is a good example of the hidden attractions a pool may hold. The

Straightforward pools have well-defined throats, bodies, and tails regardless of their shape. This perfect pool is on the Battenkill in Vermont.

curve can vary from a gentle, subtle bend to a hairpin turn. The throat of the pool in such a case can seem to flow right through the body, or it can seem to be extremely long or short. The inside of the·bend can represent the entire body of the pool, or the body can start above the bend and gently swing through the turn.

As always, the prime spots in any of these situations are at the head and tail of the pool. At the head of the pool, the water is moving faster than in the body and is also faster and deeper than the water upstream of it, which can be a rapids, a riffle, pocket water, or a run (discussed below). The throat is the most productive water even in a curving pool and usually swings to the outside of the bend in the river, which provides ideal locations for trout.

The fish in a curving pool can tuck in against bank features, out of the main current, and can easily feed on the concentrations of food the throat of the pool delivers to them. They are less likely to be line shy on the outside of the bend, but the trade-off is the difficulty in getting a good drift of the fly to them. In fact, even though it is much easier to stand on the inside of the bend and cast across to the good holding water because of the extra room you have in which to maneuver the fly rod and to cast line, proper presentation is very difficult from there because of the variety of currents your line must cross to get to the fish. It is much better to fish an outside bend from the outside shore and make straight or slightly cross-current casts either upstream or downstream.

The inside of a curving pool often holds good fish, too, because of the easy holding water close to the fertile throat water. Approach is the main problem on inside turns, as the fish are much more vulnerable and spooky in these clear, relatively featureless waters. This is a lesson it seems I must learn every spring. Not until I've seen a good

On many of the most productive trout waters, the tail of one pool quickly becomes the throat of the next, as here on Maine's Moose River.

trout scoot away from me as I stand where he had been holding do I remember to be more careful on these inside curves.

The tails of these curving pools can be as plain as in a straightforward pool, but they often curve, too, as at the throat. In addition, in a stream flowing through the irregular terrain that gives these pools their irregular shapes, the curving tails can quickly become the throats of the next pool. When this happens, the most productive waters blend as the tails merge with the throats, and this good water is broken only by the flats of the pools themselves.

The principles of approaching throats also apply to tails. Try to fish them from the shore where the water stacks up, generally on the outside of the bend.

Rapids

More often than not, pools are divided by the other important features of the river—rapids, runs, pocket water, or riffles—or by some combination of them. The water flow of these features varies from the hard, unmanageable gush of water in rapids; to the deeper, more uniform, but still strong flow of runs; to the complex but interesting and productive flow of pocket water; to the fertile flow of riffles. The velocity of the current descends in the same order, given a closely similar gradient.

The best thing that can be said about rapids is that they help pump oxygen into the water. Because of their extremely hard flow and steep gradient, to say nothing of their multiple current tongues, rapids are difficult, at best, to fish. Now and again, however, there may be pockets of water along the shore that can hold a good fish or two and where an angler can get close enough to make a short, accurate cast. Rainbows often hold in these stream-bank pockets, and northeastern anglers often focus on them when the quarry is river-run landlocked salmon.

Pools in a stream are often divided by other distinct types of flowing water, but often an angler can fish the head of a pool, its throat, and the rapid above it without changing position.

Runs

Runs are more manageable. In a run, the water from a broader section of stream narrows and therefore often picks up speed, especially if the run is on the same gradient as the water upstream. Rapids feeding into a run usually mean that the gradient has decreased as the river has narrowed. Runs also often form the throats of pools, but they can stand alone and often feed back into other moving water.

As runs narrow and deepen, they provide two strong attractions for trout. Because they are located below fertile, flowing water, where the vast majority of insect life in a stream flourishes, this forage is concentrated into the run as it is washed downstream. And because the water is deeper, and has a steadier current, fish are more protected. With protection and food available, the trout found in these runs are usually actively feeding and accept artificial flies as well as, if not better than, in any other section of the stream.

In addition, runs are the easiest moving water to fish. They have uniform, deep currents, with slick surfaces. Anglers can present their flies to the fish from a variety of angles, upstream, downstream, or across current, and they can concentrate on putting the fly in front of the fish and making it act like the natural. Rarely do you need to mend line or fight conflicting currents, and the artificial usually drifts down to feeding fish with little influence from line or leader drag.

Pocket Water and Riffles

The final two stream characteristics important to anglers are pocket water and riffles, and they're important because they are the trout's breadbasket. Myriad studies have proven that fully 80 percent of all invertebrates populating a stream are found in pocket water and riffles. They are the fertile nurseries and homes for a host of forage. And while many of these food items become concentrated in the flow of runs and at the heads of pools, both during behavioral drift and as hatching time arrives, they spend most of their lives in riffles and pocket water. Day in and day out, riffles and pocket water are the regular nutrition centers for trout, and, barring evidence of concentrated feeding activity elsewhere, fishing these areas is almost always productive. They're fun, too, as standing in good riffle or pocket water offers you a variety of spots to find trout.

Pocket water can be the most difficult feature of a river to fish, and the most productive. It is characterized by water moving over rock, gravel, and rubble streambeds punctuated by larger boulders that often, but not always, stick out of the water. These boulders cause interruptions in the flow of water that provide perfect holding lies for both resting and feeding fish, and the nature of the remaining streambed is ideal for invertebrate forage.

Fish hold in the hydraulic pocket at the head of the boulders and in the quiet waters beside and behind them. From these easy water sites, trout can either casually feast on food items that are washed into the quiet water or make quick forays into the nearby faster water.

The problem for anglers in pocket water is getting their flies to drift naturally into the holding areas of the fish. Because of the variety of currents that sweep around and through the boulders in pocket water, cross-current presentations are difficult; even slack cross-stream casts are quickly straightened out and swept downstream. But the good news is that the turbulence of the surface and the very existence of the large boulders will cloak an angler's approach, and he can often fish a much shorter line. As in other multiple-current situations, the best approach in pocket water is from directly up- or downstream, or slightly across current.

Riffles hold the same attractive numbers of invertebrates and produce the same good angling as pocket water. Trout in riffles can find plenty of holding water near the bottom where the boulders and rubble create pockets of still water. And as in pocket water, the fish can comfortably hold near this rubble and casually pick off drifting food items, or they can aggressively dart into the faster flows to feed.

The problem with riffles is that they are difficult to read. The surface is rough and broken because of the features of the riffle that are hidden on the streambed, so it is difficult to know how and where to present your artificial fly. But the more experience an angler gains in fishing riffles, the easier it becomes to unravel their mysteries.

As in other moving water, the parts of the stream that offer the trout protection from the hard flow of the current, that are relatively secure from predators, and that provide access to forage are the areas most likely to hold trout. In spite of the seemingly confused mass that the surface presents, certain of its features can tell much about the structure of the streambed. Bulges in the surface are sure indicators of subsurface boulders, which are as important to the trout in riffles as they are in pocket water. Obvious differences in the speed of the current indicate bottom structure, too, like shelves or ledges or slower side waters. And any piece of the surface that differs, even subtly, from the rest of the surface signifies some submerged feature that is likely to harbor trout.

Riffles vary in the amount of bottom structure they contain. Extremely rough surfaces indicate substantial bottom structure, and relatively calm surfaces indicate few bottom features. As a general rule, the more surface disturbance a riffle has, the more trout it will hold, because of the numerous places the fish can find safe haven and because of the numbers of forage animals that will be living on the bottom. Remember that invertebrates, crustaceans, and feed fish also need relief from the flow of the water, and places to hide, too.

An angler's experience can be measured by how well he reads riffle water. These few hints are only the beginning of what to look for. Nowhere else in the stream does experience play a more important part than in a section of riffle water. And nowhere else will an experienced angler enjoy more success.

Understanding the complexities of flowing water is a lifelong and endlessly fascinating study. Just when you thought you had a firm grasp of where trout can be found in a stream, or decided you can apply the knowledge you've gained on one stream to another, some new aspect of flowing water reveals itself to humble you.

It might be something as simple as an increase or decrease in water temperature, which can cause the trout to rearrange their priorities in favor of better water temperatures with a more comfortable oxygen content in an entirely different section of the stream. Or it might be that water levels in a particularly attractive riffle have become too high or too low for the trout. Or the tactics you've developed to fish the features of the water you're used to, whether a country brook or a western waterway, may not transfer well to a different type of water.

But one thing remains constant. Once you have discovered how interesting flowing water is, how infinitely exciting it can be when you have successfully deciphered the patterns of the trout in flowing water on a given day, you are sure to return to the challenge again and again. Flowing water is like that.

13
FISHING STILL WATER

Lakes, ponds, reservoirs, and other bodies of still water are both fascinating and frustrating to fly fishermen—fascinating because they invariably hold the biggest fish in a region, and frustrating because their flat surfaces are like a blank page to anglers trying to read their mysteries. Unlike in flowing water, where the surface reflects the structure, makeup, and depth of the water, and where fish are usually stationary, in still water little or nothing is revealed by the surface, and the fish move about to find more comfortable water temperatures and forage.

The goal for anglers on still water remains the same as on any water type, namely to present an appropriate artificial in a manner and place where the trout will take it. But while the goals are the same as on moving water, the methods of accomplishing them are quite different. Certainly attention must be paid to the native forage on which the trout concentrate, but in still water the range of forage types is more limited, and an angler intent on catching larger trout can reduce that range of forage even further. For still-water anglers, finding fish remains the most pressing problem.

Finding Fish

Anglers who do most of their trout fly-fishing on still waters know that learning about the geography of a body of water is the key to finding fish. They know, or will endeavor to find out, where the major and minor inlets are; where a lake drains; where there are shoals and bays, underwater islands, and weed lines; where there might be midlake humps or flats; where underwater springs bubble up; and everything else that might

Inlets and outlets and water flowing through are among the features to look for to find fish on a small lake.

help them isolate the most productive areas. They understand the details that are important in drainage lakes, which receive water from inlets and have a single outlet, and those that come into play on seepage lakes, where the water comes from springs or runoff and usually has only a minor outflow or none at all. They know that on newly formed lakes, reservoirs, and beaver ponds, old streambeds are at the core of water movement, and moving water means better oxygen concentration, better nutrient and forage movement, and hence higher concentrations of gamefish.

In short, mapping out the obvious and the subtle nuances of water's geography is vital to finding fish. Detailed commercial

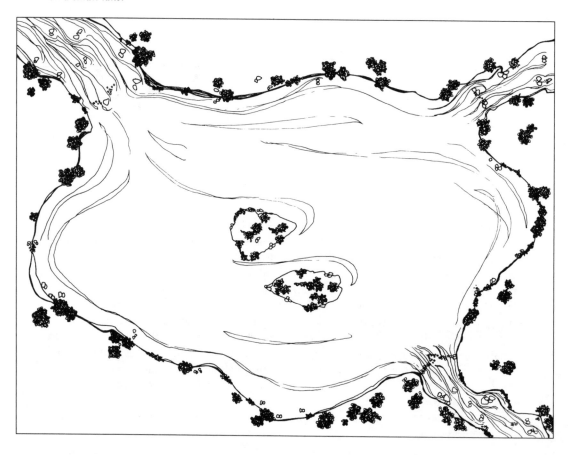

maps of these lake features are becoming available, but even without them, anglers can develop their own strategies of discovery both for new lakes and for those that are old friends. As their experience on still waters increases, it will become easier to go to specific productive sites, but as importantly, they'll be able to approach new waters with a better eye for where fish hold and how to catch them.

Ed Lofland, a veteran of nearly 60 years of angling and my father-in-law, has always amazed me with his ability to find fish on lakes and ponds. His directions to me for positioning the boat or canoe are precise, and he has even had me turn the boat completely around so that his end was where my end had been. And he always outfishes me.

I've pressed him for years to reveal his secrets, and occasionally he opens up with something about a sunken log, or the deepest spot in a pond, or the location of an underwater spring. Usually, though, he just tells me, "Been here before." But even on new water, Ed will have me tour the pond and then direct me where to anchor. And we'll usually start catching trout. At least Ed will.

The best places to start looking for still-water fish are the most obvious ones. John Merwin, in his excellent slim book *Streamer-Fly Fishing*, gave a succinct guide to finding fish in still water: "The best still water fishing," he said, "is usually where the water isn't still at all." And the most obvious moving water in lakes and ponds is at the inlets and outlets.

INLETS

Even in these obvious locales, important differences should be noted. At inlets, the smorgasbord of food that trout seek is more varied than almost anywhere else in the lake. Not only are there the standard feed fish and crustaceans that find forage in the incoming flow of water, but many of the food items that form the backbone of nutri-

Inlets on water of any size are fertile forage and gamefish areas. On Massachusetts' huge Quabbin Reservoir this is a prime spot for landlocked salmon in the early spring and again in the fall.

tion in rivers and streams are washed into the lake as well. During periods of high insect activity in the stream, such as before and during major hatches of mayflies and caddis, many subaquatic food items are washed into the lake to entice the trout there, too.

In the shoal areas that fan out from and are adjacent to an incoming water flow, fertile habitats exist for a host of organisms. The high oxygen content and the shallowness of these waters provide great places for a variety of insects, minnows, sculpins, and darters to concentrate. In addition, these incoming waters attract migrant fish intent on passing through the lake or just going upstream to spawn. No New Englander would ever pass up a good inflow of water when the smelt are running in the spring, and alewives, young eels, young trout, and the like are often congregating near and moving into inlet streams.

All these forage attract trout, and attract

them in good numbers and sizes. When the added attraction of cooler water temperatures in the summer and more highly oxygenated water year-round are considered, it is easy to see why inlets are important throughout the angling year.

Outlets

Outlets are more subtly attractive. Larger trout are more likely to concentrate there, if only because the organisms coming upstream

Active beaver ponds are especially fertile spots because of the nutrients they expose, the insect life they support, and the good trout that inevitably are drawn to their waters.

and into the lake, and migrating out of it, too, are more likely to be larger and more of a mouthful for the bigger trout. As we've seen before, larger fish need larger forage, and the concentration of larger forage at outlets explains their attraction. The angling action at an outlet will probably be less consistent than at an inlet, where a variety of sizes of gamefish forage for a variety of food, but the size of the fish will be largest at the outlet.

Old Streambeds

On newer lakes, such as reservoirs and impoundments, on smaller lakes with large quantities of water flowing in and out, and on beaver ponds, water will move where the old

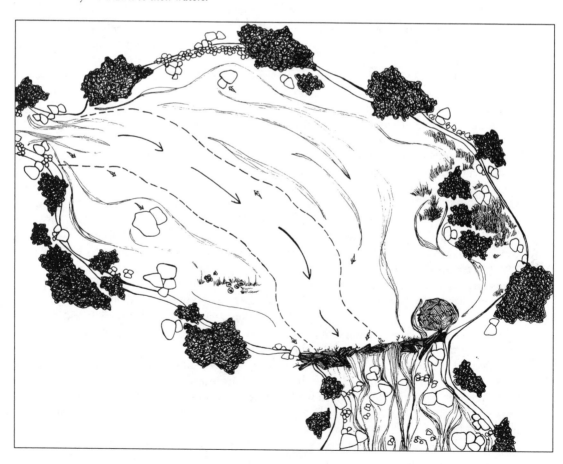

streambed was gouged out. Again, the attraction of moving water is its fertility, oxygen content, and temperature. The fertility supports whole colonies of nutrients on which nearly every living organism in any water is based, on up the food chain to gamefish.

Identifying where these old streambeds meander is not difficult in smaller, well-defined waters. The course of the stream was probably a fairly direct route from inlet to outlet. Even if the old stream did meander some, the flow of attractive water will follow a fairly direct route along the deepest sections of a small lake or beaver pond.

When the water is larger, say in a reservoir, the problem becomes more difficult, but the solution is easier than you might guess. On larger bodies of water, the streambed will still follow the deepest sections of the impoundment, but at a certain depth, which varies according to the time of year and the water temperature, the water pressure and temperature literally squeeze the oxygen out of the water. Below the famous thermocline, there will rarely be any forage or fish living, regardless of the way the old streambed directs the flow of water. There is, therefore, a practical limit to how far out into a lake an old streambed remains productive. In addition, there is a practical limit to the depth at which fly fishermen can fish. Most of us find that limit to be about 30 to 35 feet.

Finding and fishing the old streambeds of these newer bodies of water, then, means concentrating on the more manageable sections of water. Out in the major sections of the lake, the water is probably too deep to hold trout that will be focusing on food anyway, but in closer to shore, in the bays and setbacks and near the inlets, finding and fishing the old riverbed becomes easier as you reduce a vast water to its components. Certainly a map of the impoundment before it was flooded will eliminate much of the guess-

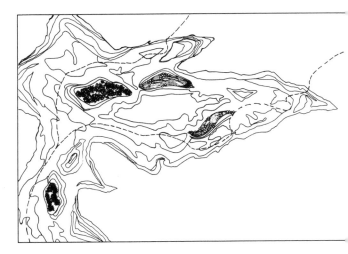

The vast expanses of flat water on larger lakes and reservoirs can be broken down into their components and their productive spots isolated.

work, but by systematically covering the water in a smaller area of the lake, you can home in on the streambed, for that's where most of the feeding fish will be. As you catch more fish on more excursions, you'll see a pattern to where they are holding and be able to determine where the old streambed lies.

OTHER BOTTOM FEATURES

Most smaller ponds and lakes have fairly uniform bottoms, where the shores taper down to the deepest water, be it an old streambed or the center of the body of water. But the larger a body of water, the more likely it is to have an irregular bottom. Submerged islands and underwater humps may well up from the bottom, extensive flats may be surrounded by deeper waters, and piles of debris left by receding glaciers may leave a variety of features on the bottom of a cold-water lake.

These places become important to anglers because, like the other fertile features of a body of water, they attract the underwater life that in turn attracts gamefish.

They combine the elements that help forage survive, namely, cover, optimal water temperature and fertility, sunlight, and oxygen content. When the water depth, clarity, and fertility are right, a microcosm of the entire life and food cycle exists.

Weed lines and other underwater vegetation can be the most important feature of certain lakes and ponds. This is true for two basic reasons. First, the weeds may provide the best or the only cover for forage. They spend most of their lives darting in and among the protective vegetation, and the trout cruise the edges of the weeds chasing these food items. The second reason is that in many bodies of water, these weeds are the homes and nurseries of a variety of important insects and crustaceans. Scuds and sowbugs, in particular, thrive in these weeds, and damselflies and dragonflies won't be far from them either. And where there is an abundance of feed, trout won't be far away.

All the preceding lake features are permanent, identifiable areas that can be physically discovered and pinpointed. Once they've been found, it would be a waste of good fishing time to have to rediscover them every time out, so keeping a detailed record of their location only makes good sense. Whether or not you're carrying a map of the water, make precise notes of what you've discovered and where. Triangulate each time you've discovered an important detail, and be sure to note the shore features you are using to pinpoint your location, as well as the details of the underwater feature.

DEPTHFINDERS

While some fly-fishing purists might cringe at the idea, modern sonar depthfinders can reduce searching time for the underwater features of a lake to a minimum. While many of these units have an astounding array of bells and whistles, and are often touted as "fish finders," I've always maintained that their best use is for revealing bottom features and water depth. They can be extremely useful for revealing all the features described so far in this chapter, and when those details have been noted on paper, leave the portable sonar unit at home if you like. But remember, the idea is to be fishing, not looking for good places to fish, so don't discount the utility of modern technologies.

UNDERWATER SPRINGS

One feature that eludes sonar, has no identifying, visible characteristics, and has made many an angler or guide seem a head above the competition, is the precise knowledge of where underwater springs enrich the bottom of a body of still water. These inflows of rich, uniformly cold water can concentrate the trout populations of a lake or pond, especially if the surrounding water is either colder or warmer than optimal trout water temperatures. Many anglers know that during the height of summer, trout seek out cool-water

Spring-fed ponds and lakes keep fish growing year-round. This nice rainbow came from East Newton Lake in Wyoming, a spring-fed body of water.

inlets and springs. Of the two, the underwater springs are the more attractive because of their consistently cooler waters. But these springs also attract trout very early in the season because their water is warmer than the surrounding frigid waters, and at that time, the trout will stay close to springs.

Pinpointing underwater springs is a bit trickier than finding specific features of the underwater landscape. There is no typical spot in a lake for a spring. They can flow in from the edges of the shore, from the depths, or from anywhere in between. If the springs are near shore, or feed into the lake as a small inlet, then the luxuriant foliage on the shore will be markedly more lush during the height of summer. But springs that are farther out in the water must be meticulously searched for and noted. They reveal themselves by the number of fish they give up, either to you as you explore, or to other anglers. If you see a concentration of canoes or boats in a particular area on a hot July day, there's probably a cold spring seep nearby. Note it carefully on your map or in your log book, because it may well be the only place that will give up fish in the heat of summer.

In addition, that sonar unit you may have used to map the lake bottom often comes with a thermometer built into the transducer mounted to the transom. Its best use is finding those pockets of fertile, cold water that well up from a lake bottom. If you have an aversion to these technologies, at least trail a standard stream thermometer along and check it periodically.

STRATIFICATION

Where the fish will be found in a body of still water is a function of all the physical characteristics just covered and of the temperatures of that body of water.

Few anglers are unaware that lakes stratify as the year progresses. In short, this means that the lake will eventually divide into three layers of water temperatures as summer arrives and peaks. The upper layer, the epilimnion, contains the warmest water, but also the highest oxygen content. It can be a fairly thick layer of water, often more than 30 feet deep, particularly during a long spell of hot weather. The second layer is the thermocline. It is a thin transitional layer, rarely more than 5 or 6 feet deep, where temperatures and oxygen content drop. The third layer is the water below the thermocline, the hypolimnion, that holds the coldest water but also has little, if any, oxygen.

This stratification is pertinent to anglers only on large, deep bodies of water and only in summer. On smaller, shallower lakes and ponds, the warming of the water is usually uniform since the wave action, the inflow and outflow of water, and the effects of daylight and dark continually mix the water.

On those larger bodies of water that do stratify, the thermocline usually forms at between 30 and 60 feet of water, and the fish find their most comfortable water just above it, where water temperatures and oxygen content are optimal. Again, because of atmospheric conditions, wave action, water flows, and day and night thermal fluctuations, the thermocline varies from week to week, from day to day, and even during the course of a day. However, where the thermocline coincides with a lake's structure, active gamefish mix with prey, and the fishing is usually good.

The point of this discussion of water temperatures and stratification is that still-water anglers need the know-how to present their flies at different depths. In early spring, trout and forage seek the warming waters near the surface and in the shallows. Later in the spring and during early summer, before stratification has occurred, fish can be found in the largest variety of depths. During summer, on smaller waters the continual mix of water temperatures again means that fish can be found at most depths, and where stratification does occur, that narrow range of comfortable water temperatures will vary. In late summer and autumn, the cycle reverses.

Still-Water Tackle and Gear

The vast majority of productive fly-fishing on still waters is done subsurface. On some lakes and ponds with the appropriate bottom sediment, there may be some fishable hatches, particularly for hexagenia mayflies, some of the Drakes, and a few caddis. Even then, however, the best angling may be just below the surface with emerger patterns. By and large, still waters will mean getting a subsurface fly down to a depth where the fish are holding and feeding.

Because of this, a full-sinking fly line on an appropriately balanced outfit is essential. In general, sinking fly lines are rated by the number of inches the line will sink per second. The trade-off is that the faster the line sinks, the higher its density is and the heavier it is per foot. This means that lines with a sink rate as high as 7½ inches per second would require a 14- or 15-weight rod to cast them, a real brute if you plan to cast all day. More appropriate would be a line with a sink rate of 5 to 6 inches per second, which would balance with an 8- or 9-weight rod.

In addition, innovative lines are now available that ensure a uniform sink rate for the entire length of the line. They are called *density-compensated* lines, and their entire length has the same weight per foot in all sections, including the thinner tip of the line, the thicker belly, and the thinner taper toward the rod end. These lines prevent a faster-sinking belly from forming in the mid-

On lakes and ponds, sink-tip or, preferably, full-sinking lines can be especially helpful in locating the depths at which fish are holding.

dle of the line, which would pull the fly down deeper in midretrieve and then back up at the end of the retrieve. Consistent depth of the fly during the retrieve is important, and these new lines solve a problem that has long plagued still-water anglers.

The best taper for the fly line is either a weight-forward or shooting taper. The sinking part of these lines is out front, and is followed by a thinner section that won't tend to raise the line up through the water. We'll see why this is important in the next section on presentation. More importantly, both of these lines allow maximum-distance casting, making it possible to cover more water with each cast. The leader on this sinking line outfit should be relatively short, say 6 to 7 feet, again because we want the fly to follow along at the same depth as the fly line. A long tapered leader would tend to float the fly higher than the running depth of the fly line.

Most still-water fishing is done from some sort of surface craft, be it a float tube, canoe, jonboat, McKenzie boat, or standard boat. Certainly much angling is also done by wading. But for subsurface fishing on still water, an angler wants to be as high off the water as he can, and for two good reasons. First, to cover as much water as possible, he has to make the longest casts he can consistently and comfortably make. Standing up in a boat works best. Second, when striking fish, he needs as much leverage above the water as he can get. The slack in his line in the standard L-shaped presentation discussed below means that he'll need plenty of above-water leverage to set the hook.

So it is best to use a boat whenever possible. But when access for a trailer and boat is absent, I much prefer a canoe over a float tube because a canoe keeps you higher off of the water. Canoes and float tubes are about the same in portability and cost; a 13-foot canoe weighs in at 40 pounds or less, and a used one costs less than $200.

Canoes have a long history in still-water angling. They allow quiet approach to fertile sections of water, and their low gunwales give the angler plenty of room from which to make his cast.

Presentation

Effective still-water presentation means covering all the water likely to hold fish. While this sounds relatively simple, it is actually more complex than stream fishing because you need to cover not only the target surface area but also the entire range of depths in that target area, at least until you've discovered at which depth active fish are holding.

The tried-and-true method for doing this is the circular countdown method. With your boat or canoe anchored fore and aft to prevent it from turning in the wind, start at a specific spot, say the bow of the boat or toward some specific shoreline feature. Cast out your maximum length of line, and retrieve your fly just under the surface on all your casts. Complete a full circle with this retrieve around the boat.

On your next series of casts, count a specific number of seconds, say 5 or 10, before you begin your retrieve. Because you know the sink rate of your fly line, say 6 inches per second, you'll know that a 5-second count will put your fly down 2½ feet; a 10 count, 5 feet; and so on. Make your maximum cast each time so that you will cover the water thoroughly, both the surface area and the depth.

An important detail that I first saw described by Ken Allen in an *American Angler* article several years ago helps keep the fly line and the fly at the same depth throughout the retrieve. As the fly line is sinking, said Allen, play out some slack line so that it descends straight down from the rod tip. The line from the cast to the rod tip then forms an L, and when you retrieve your fly, it stays at the same depth, rather than returning at a diagonal up through the water. The method lets you know at exactly which depth a fish strikes, regardless of whether he hits out at the end of the cast or close to the boat. Then you can maintain that depth with subsequent casts.

Water clarity and the distance of your cast will help you decide how close each cast needs to be to the last one, that is, how many casts you need to make in one full circle around the boat. Experience helps, too. In clear water, a fish can see your fly from greater distances, so you can make fewer, more widely separated casts. If you are a proficient caster, regularly throwing out 80 to 90 feet of line, you'll need to make more casts because you're covering a larger circle. As water clarity decreases, you'll need to make more casts, too, since the fish can't see your fly as well. And clarity affects how deep you should allow each cycle of casts to sink. In clear water, 5-foot increments are probably most effective, but that number decreases as the water becomes less clear.

There are three more factors to consider. The first is the speed of your retrieve and its action. Generally a steady stripping of line is best when you are searching for fish. This keeps your line at the same depth, gives plenty of motion to your fly, and helps you discover at which depth the fish are holding. If you are sure you have fish at a set depth in a particular spot, and they aren't taking, you may want to vary your retrieve, going faster or slower and pausing now and again to give lifelike action to your fly.

The second factor is the type of fly you have on the end of your line. A good working knowledge of what's available on a particular body of water is invaluable, but there is always a variety of forage on which fish will feed, so be prepared with a good variety of flies. Cover the water thoroughly with your preferred fly, but if it doesn't produce after a reasonable time, don't hesitate to change it. (See "What to Use" below.)

The third variable, of course, is location. Even if you have had steady action at a location before, say on a submerged sandbar, and you are confident the fish will be there, they might not be. If they aren't, change your location, and change the type of structure you are fishing, too. If the fish aren't on a sandbar in the north end of the lake, they probably won't be on a sandbar in the south end of the lake, either. So when you try a new spot, try a different feature, say an inlet or the outlet, a weed line, or some rubble bottom.

When you fish submerged structure, like underwater shoals, islands, sandbars, or weed beds, you should alter your basic approach some. Ray Bergman in *Trout* described the method clearly and logically. In shallower subsurface structure, cast only a half arc around the boat into the shallower water, with your boat anchored in the deeper water. If the fish are present and feeding, you won't scare them away by motoring or

Still waters are drawing more and more anglers to their shores because the mysteries of fishing them are beginning to be unraveled, and because they inevitably hold the largest fish in a region.

paddling into their midst. Use the same countdown method until you've covered the water you can reach, then reposition until you've covered all the shallower water. If you haven't made contact with the fish, again reposition the boat, this time in the shallower water, and cast out into the depths. Fish like the slopes leading into the shallows, and you can cover the depths appropriately, again using the countdown method and fishing all the water down to and along the slope.

What to Use

Knowledge of the favorite and secondary forage in still water is invaluable. It is as important as knowing that a certain stream is a hotbed of caddis activity but contains no stoneflies. Where that knowledge comes from is immaterial. Only tight-lipped, anti-social Yankees would insist on personally discovering what a body of water holds for forage, so if you are new to a water, ask questions. Ask them at the local fly-fishing shop, at the bait store, and of the fish and game biologists. Ask friends and strangers. As you'll notice, some of the very best anglers in the country are exceptionally gregarious, and all the while they're enjoying their friendly chats, they're accumulating knowledge too, usually about forage and fly patterns, but also about hot spots, best times, and yes, even about where to find the best deli to buy lunch.

Armed with the best information you can glean, add to it by being observant and logical. Observe what's in and around the water you are fishing. Plenty of dragon- or dam-

selflies? Get out some of your big nymphs. Mayflies or caddis coming off at dawn or dusk? Same thing. Nymphs on the bottom might be productive, or emergers in the top foot or so might produce. Need a cool spot for lunch? Paddle into an outlet or over the shallows and see what kind of life is there. Shiners? What type? Dace or sculpins? Smelt or trout fry? Are there leeches in the water? Crayfish? Scuds and sowbugs? Make note and match what's available.

Then, with that information, use logic to decide how to fish the water. With showing and dimpling trout, you can cast to the rings of the rises with relatively stationary flies that imitate the insects that are common in the lake or pond. But when you don't have the trout on the surface and you have to cover water, you'll need a fly that accepts and is accentuated by the motion of the retrieve. Many of the flies covered in the chapters on swimming nymphs, streamers and bucktails, and the soft swimmers absolutely come alive when they are worked through the water. Match them to what you've discovered about the water and you'll do well.

Still waters present a new set of mysteries to be unraveled and require new methods to be learned, but their reward is often the biggest trout a region has to offer. The fishing may seem quite different from stream fishing, with reading flowing water and focusing on matching the hatch, but the goal is the same, namely, to take trout on flies. Once the mysteries are understood and the methods mastered, many good fly fishermen look first to still waters for their best fishing.

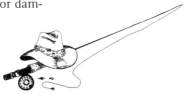

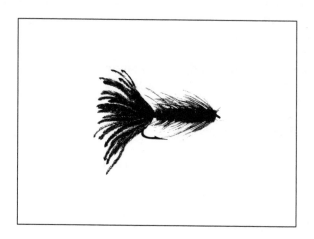

14
FAVORITE FLY PATTERNS

An angler's fly-tying evolves much as his enjoyment of fly-fishing does. Early in his career it is comforting to fish a particular fly that
works particularly well at a particular time,
say a Hendrickson Nymph during the first
week of May. It is also gratifying to use Hendrickson Nymphs that you have put together
yourself, and fly-tyers will suggest that the
best way to learn the craft of fly-tying is to use
proven methods to construct classic patterns.

As an angler's experience grows, at the
bench and on the stream, he will inevitably
expand on the patterns he ties and on his
own interpretations of those patterns, as he
will experiment with the places he fishes
and the methods he tries. Throughout his
lifetime he will be fascinated with the materials he uses in his flies and the way they

are put onto a hook, and by the apparently
infinite enjoyment he can derive from trout
and the places where they live.

What follows then is a listing of fly patterns, some ancient, some classic, and some
fairly new, that provide a jumping-off point
for fly-tyers (most are shown on the color
plates, between pages 86 and 87). They certainly provide the basis for new tyers to expand on the patterns in their fly boxes. And
perhaps they'll present some new ideas to
veteran tyers. But as we evolve as anglers
and tyers, let's keep in mind that none of
these patterns are etched in stone. Please
try your own ideas with them. As new materials become available, or as you gain new
appreciation for old ones, by all means experiment. That's where the classic patterns

were born, and it's where the classics of the future will come from.

The patterns below are listed with their most basic descriptions. Because the variety of available materials is everchanging, use those available to you that accomplish the desired effect. Hooks are described generically—nymph, wet-fly, streamer, and so forth—because manufacturers are constantly coming out with improved shapes, sharper points, barbless hooks, and hooks with more specialized uses. While the Mustad 3906 has been the standard wet-fly and nymph hook for years, many manufacturers, like Tiemco, Partridge, Eagle Claw, and even Mustad itself, have all come out with more specialized hooks. Use what works best for you.

Mayfly Nymphs

Note:
- *For deep-floating nymphs add wraps of weight to thorax.*
- *For emerging nymphs tie on light-wire hooks.*
- *For swimming nymphs eliminate wing cases, tie in the round, and encircle the head with soft hackle, one or two turns.*

GOLD-RIBBED HARE'S EAR NYMPH (PLATE 1 AND ABOVE)
Size: 8–14
Thread: brown
Tail: woodduck flank-feather barbs
Abdomen/thorax: hare's ear fur
Rib: gold oval tinsel
Wing case: dark turkey
Legs: picked out from thorax

HENDRICKSON NYMPH (PLATE 1)
Size: 12–16
Thread: brown
Tail: woodduck flank feathers
Abdomen/thorax: red/brown dubbing
Rib: copper wire
Wing case: black turkey-quill segment
Legs: brown partridge barbules

CAHILL NYMPH (PLATE 1)
Size: 12–14
Thread: tan
Tail: woodduck barbules
Abdomen: tan/amber dubbing
Thorax: mottled tan/amber dubbing
Rib: tan monocord
Wing case: light turkey quill
Legs: woodduck barbules

OLIVE-BROWN NYMPH (PLATE 1)
Size: 18–24
Thread: dark olive
Tail: pheasant-tail barbules
Abdomen/thorax: olive/brown dubbing
Rib: dark olive floss
Wing case: dark goose quill
Legs: dark dun barbules

TRICO NYMPH (PLATE 1)
Size: 18–24
Thread: black
Tail: blue dun barbules
Abdomen/thorax: black
Wing case: black quill
Legs: blue dun barbules

Potamanthus Nymph (Plate 1)
Size: 10–12, 3X long
Thread: brown
Tail: pheasant-tail barbules
Abdomen/thorax: yellow/amber fur
Rib: oval gold tinsel
Wing case: brown turkey-quill segment
Legs: woodduck barbules
Note: For gills add grouse philoplumes to sides of abdomen before ribbing.

March Brown Nymph (Plate 1)
Size: 8–12
Thread: brown
Tail: pheasant-tail barbules
Abdomen/thorax: tan/amber fur
Rib: brown monocord
Wing case: dark turkey-quill segment
Legs: brown partridge barbules

Green Drake Nymph (Plate 1)
Size: 8–12
Thread: olive
Tail: pheasant-tail barbules
Abdomen/thorax: golden olive fur
Rib: olive monocord
Wing case: dark turkey-quill segment
Legs: woodduck barbules

Pheasant Tail Nymph (Plate 1)
Size: 12–20
Thread: brown
Tail: pheasant-tail barbules
Abdomen: pheasant barbules wrapped
Thorax: peacock herl
Rib: copper wire
Wing case: pheasant-tail barbules
Legs: pheasant-tail barbules

Tellico (Plate 1)
Size: 10–16
Thread: black
Tail: brown hackle barbules
Abdomen/thorax: yellow floss
Rib: peacock herl
Shellback: peacock herl from tail to head
Legs: brown hackle

Zug Bug (Plate 1)
Size: 8–16
Thread: black
Tail: peacock swords
Body: peacock herl
Rib: oval silver tinsel
Wing case: mallard flank feather
Legs: brown hackle

Whitlock's Red Squirrel (Plate 1)
Size: 6–18
Thread: black
Tail: red squirrel
Abdomen: red squirrel belly (light)
Thorax: red squirrel back (dark)
Rib: copper wire
Legs: brown soft grizzly hackle

Brooks' Ida May (Plate 1)
Size: 8–10
Thread: black
Tail: green grizzly-hackle barbules
Abdomen/thorax: fuzzy black yarn
Rib: peacock herl and gold wire
Legs: grizzly hackle collar

Gartside's Sparrow (Plate 1)
Size: 6–14, 2X or 3X long
Thread: olive
Tail: pheasant-tail marabou
Body: olive rabbit and gray squirrel
Hackle: pheasant tail with barbs to bend
Collar: pheasant-tail marabou

Caddis Larvae and Pupae

BREADCRUST (PLATE 2)
Size: 8–16
Thread: orange
Body: rusty orange fur
Rib: brown monocord
Legs: soft brown grizzly hackle

BRASSIE (PLATE 2)
Size: 12–20
Thread: black
Body: brass or copper wire
Head: black or gray fur

CADDIS GILLED LARVA (PLATE 2)
Size: 12–20
Thread: black
Body: Larva Lace or similar (variety of colors)
Rib: ostrich herl, counterwound with copper wire for durability
Head: brown or black dubbing
Legs: grizzly hackle barbules

FUR CADDIS LARVA (PLATE 2)
Size: 10–20
Thread: brown
Body: fur (olive, green, yellow)
Head: dark brown/black fur
Legs: woodduck barbules

SPARKLE PUPA (PLATE 2)
Size: 12–18
Thread: brown to yellow
Body: fur and Antron yarn (variety of colors)
Overbody: long Antron fibers tied in at bend and pulled back over body
Head: brown fur
Legs: partridge barbules
*Note: For **Deep Sparkle Pupa** add weight under body. For **Sparkle Pupa Emerger** use no weight, and leave some Antron fibers trailing behind hook. Some folks add short deer-hair wings for emergers. Use a variety of body and Antron colors for all Sparkle Pupa patterns: yellow, bright green, olive, tan, ginger.*

FUR CADDIS PUPA (PLATE 2)
Size: 8–14
Thread: brown
Body: brown dubbing
Wings: dark quills, short and stubby
Head: dark brown dubbing
Legs: picked-out fur
Note: Tie both the Fur Caddis Pupa, above, and Solomon's Caddis Pupa, below, on dry-fly hooks for effective emerging caddis pupae. Add short deer-hair wings to top of hook just behind the eye for extra effect.

SOLOMON'S CADDIS PUPA
Size: 12–18
Thread: brown
Body: olive green or dark dubbing
Rib: brown monocord
Wings: dark quills, short and stubby
Head: peacock herl
Legs: partridge barbules

BORGER'S WET/DRY FLY (PLATE 2)
Size: 12–24
Thread: to match body
Body: dubbed fur (variety of colors from light olive to olive to green to tan to brown)
Hackle collar: grouse, partridge, starling, or woodcock (match size to hook size)

Stonefly Nymphs

Brooks' Montana Stone (Plate 4)
Size: 4–8, 3X to 4X long
Thread: black
Tail: six crow barbules
Abdomen/thorax: black fuzzy yarn
Rib: copper wire
Legs: grizzly and brown grizzly, wound over thorax
Gills: gray ostrich next to legs

Brooks' Yellow Stone (Plate 4)
Size: 4–10, 3X to 4X long
Thread: brown
Tail: light turkey barbules
Abdomen/thorax: yellow/brown yarn
Rib 1: gold yarn wound backward and forward
Rib 2: gold wire
Legs: grizzly and brown grizzly, wound over thorax
Gills: gray or white ostrich next to legs

Whitlock's Black Stone (Plate 4)
Size: 2–4, 3X to 4X long
Thread: black
Tail: black goose biots
Abdomen: black sparkle dubbing
Abdomen rib: copper wire
Abdomen back: black nylon raffia
Thorax/head: brown sparkle dubbing
Legs: brown hen grizzly on top of thorax
Wing case/top of head: black nylon raffia
Antennae: black goose biots
Note: Adjust colors and hook sizes for **Golden Stone** *(4–6),* **Orange Stone** *(8–10),* **Olive Stone** *(12–14),* **Yellow Stone** *(10–12), but use same procedures.*

Montana (Plate 4)
Size: 4–12, 3X long
Thread: black
Tail: black goose biots
Abdomen: yellow chenille
Thorax: black chenille
Wing case: black chenille
Legs: black hackle over thorax

Bitch Creek (Plate 4)
Size: 4–12, 3X long
Thread: black
Tail: white rubber hackle
Abdomen: woven orange and black chenille
Thorax: black chenille
Legs: brown hackle
Antennae: white rubber hackle

Albino Stone (Plate 4)
Size: 4–12, 3X to 4X long
Thread: white
Tail: teal flank barbules
Rib: white monocord
Abdomen/thorax: off-white fur
Wing case/head: tan mottled turkey-quill segment
Legs: grizzly
Antennae: mottled turkey biots

Eastern Yellow Stone (Plate 4)
Size: 6–10, 3X long
Thread: yellow
Tail: woodduck barbules
Rib: gold floss and gold wire
Abdomen/thorax: yellow amber fur
Wing case/head: tan mottled turkey-quill segment
Legs: ginger grizzly
Antennae: mottled turkey biots

Streamers

GRAY GHOST (PLATE 3)
Size: 2–6, 6X to 8X long
Thread: black
Body: orange floss ribbed with flat silver tinsel
Wing: peacock herl, over which is a golden pheasant crest curving down, then four gray saddle hackles
Throat: sparse white bucktail and a short golden pheasant crest
Shoulders: silver pheasant body feather
Cheeks: jungle cock

NINE-THREE (PLATE 3)
Size: 2–6, 4X to 8X long
Thread: black
Body: flat silver tinsel or Mylar tubing
Wing: sparse white bucktail, over which are two green saddle hackles tied flat and two black saddle hackles tied conventionally over the top of the green hackles (green and black marabou may be used instead)

BLACK GHOST (PLATE 3)
Size: 2–12, 4X to 8X long
Thread: black
Tail: yellow hackle barbules
Body: black floss or wool ribbed with flat silver tinsel, or black Mylar tubing
Throat: yellow hackle barbules
Wing: four white saddle hackles, or white bucktail, or white marabou, or a white zonker strip
Cheeks: jungle cock

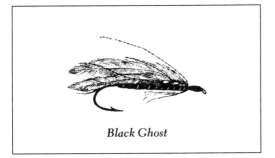

Black Ghost

MAGOG SMELT (PLATE 3)
Size: 2–6, 6X to 8X long
Thread: black
Body: flat silver tinsel or silver Mylar tubing
Wing: white then yellow then lavender bucktail topped by four to six strands of peacock herl
Throat: red hackle barbs
Shoulders: teal flank feathers

BLACK-NOSED DACE (PLATE 3)
Size: 4–12, 3X to 4X long
Thread: black
Tail: red yarn
Body: flat silver tinsel ribbed with oval silver tinsel, or silver Mylar tubing
Wing: white then black then brown bucktail, tied sparse

MITCHELL CREEK (PLATE 3)
Size: 4–10, 6X long
Thread: red
Body: silver Mylar tubing
Wing: gray marabou
Throat: white marabou
Head: gray and white marabou tied forward of the eye and then pulled back over the hook shank to form a bullet-shaped head
Gills: red thread
Eyes: yellow with black pupil
*Note: This is the **Mitchell Creek Gray Ghost**. Try the **Mitchell Creek Black Ghost**, **Nine-three**, **Red and White**, and others. As a variation, add colored or holographic Mylar fibers to the head and wings.*

JOE'S SMELT (PLATE 3)
Size: 2–6, 6X long
Thread: black
Tail: red hackle barbs
Body: silver Mylar tubing tied at back with red thread
Throat: red paint
Wing: pintail flank feather tied flat
Head: black with yellow eye and black pupil
*Note: **Jerry's Smelt** is the same fly but with a pearlescent Mylar body.*

MUDDLER MINNOW (PLATE 3)

Size: 2–16
Thread: brown
Tail: mottled tan turkey-quill sections
Body: flat gold tinsel
Wing: gray squirrel tail, over which are mottled tan turkey-quill sections
Head and collar: natural deer body hair, spun and clipped to form head, leaving flared hair as a collar back over the body
*Note: The variations of the Muddler Minnow seem endless and include the **Marabou Muddler** in a rainbow of colors, the **Bucktail Muddler Minnow**, and the **Multicolor Muddler**.*

MICKEY FINN

Size: 2–12, 3X to 6X long
Thread: black
Body: flat silver tinsel ribbed with oval silver tinsel, or silver Mylar tubing
Wing: yellow then red then yellow bucktail

RED AND WHITE BUCKTAIL

Size: 2–12, 3X to 6X long
Thread: black
Body: flat silver tinsel with oval silver ribbing, or silver Mylar tubing
Wing: white then red bucktail topped with four to eight strands of peacock herl

CARDINELLE (PLATE 3)

Size: 2–10, 4X to 6X long
Thread: hot orange
Body: fluorescent red or orange wool
Wing: fluorescent red or orange nylon hair, over which is red marabou
Hackle: yellow, long, collar style

MATUKA SCULPIN (PLATE 3)

Size: 2–8, 4X to 6X long
Thread: olive
Body: olive yarn
Rib: oval gold tinsel
Throat: red yarn
Wing and tail: four olive grizzly saddle hackles tied matuka (matuku) style
Pectoral fins: olive-speckled hen body feathers
Collar: olive deer body hair over top half of hook
Head: spun olive deer body hair

WOOLY WORM (PLATE 3)

Size: 2–12, 2X to 4X long
Thread: to match body color
Tail: red wool
Body: black, brown, olive, or yellow chenille
Hackle: natural grizzly or to match body color, palmered
Note: Wooly Worms and Woolly Buggers can also be tied with a range of crystal chenille colors for the body.

WOOLLY BUGGER (PLATE 3)

Size: 2–14, 3X or 4X long
Thread: to match body color
Tail: marabou to match body color
Body: tan, brown, black olive, or yellow chenille
Hackle: natural grizzly or to match body color, palmered

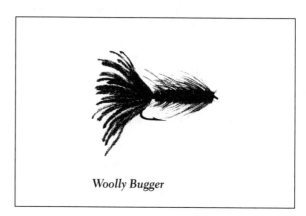

Woolly Bugger

Wet Flies

LEISENRING BLACK GNAT (PLATE 2)
Size: 14–16
Thread: crimson
Body: black floss or barbules from crow's wing feather
Collar: purple-hued black feather from starling

LEISENRING GRAY HACKLE (PLATE 2)
Size: 12–14
Thread: primrose yellow
Body: bronze peacock herl
Rib: gold tinsel
Collar: furnace hackle, light

LEISENRING IRON BLUE DUN (PLATE 2)
Size: 12–14
Thread: crimson
Tail: honey dun hackle barbules
Body: gray mole fur, thin
Collar: honey dun hackle

PARTRIDGE AND GREEN (PLATE 2)
Size: 12–16
Thread: black
Body: bright green floss
Thorax: sparse hare's ear dubbing
Collar: partridge or grouse
Note: This is the basic design for the ancient soft hackles, often tied without the thorax. Floss colors vary, but orange and yellow are also favorites.

COACHMAN (PLATE 2)
Size: 8–16
Thread: black
Tag: flat gold tinsel
Body: peacock herl
Rib: gold wire
Hackle: dark brown
Wing: white duck quill
*Note: **Leadwing Coachman** uses gray quills.*

LIGHT CAHILL
Size: 8–16
Thread: cream
Tail: woodduck flank barbules
Body: cream fur
Hackle: light ginger
Wing: woodduck flank feather

DARK CAHILL (PLATE 2)
Size: 10–14
Thread: black
Tail: woodduck barbules
Body: dark gray fur
Hackle: dark ginger
Wing: woodduck flank feather

PALE EVENING DUN
Size: 12–16
Thread: gray
Tail: light dun hackle barbules
Body: pale yellow fur
Hackle: light dun hen
Wing: light gray duck quill

COW DUNG
Size: 10–14
Thread: black
Tag: flat gold tinsel
Body: olive fur
Hackle: dark ginger hen
Wing: tan duck quill

ALDER (PLATE 2)
Size: 10–14
Thread: black
Tag: flat gold tinsel
Body: peacock herl
Hackle: black hen
Wing: tan turkey wing quill

ROYAL COACHMAN (PLATE 2)
Size: 10–16
Thread: black
Tail: golden pheasant tippets
Body: peacock herl, red floss, peacock herl
Hackle: Coachman brown
Wing: white duck quill

PROFESSOR (PLATE 2)
Size: 8–16
Thread: black
Tail: red hackle barbules
Body: yellow floss
Rib: flat gold tinsel
Hackle: brown
Wing: mallard flank barbules

PARMACHENE BELLE (PLATE 2)
Size: 8–14
Thread: black
Tail: red and white hackle barbules
Body: yellow floss
Rib: flat gold tinsel
Hackle: red and white
Wing: white then red then white duck
    quill, married

MONTREAL (PLATE 2)
Size: 8–16
Thread: black
Tail: claret hackle barbules
Body: claret floss
Rib: flat gold tinsel
Hackle: claret
Wing: mottled turkey wing quill

Other Subsurface or Damp Flies

GRIFFITH'S GNAT (PLATE 1)
Size: 14–22
Thread: black
Body: peacock herl
Hackle: grizzly, palmered
Rib: gold wire

MIDGE PUPA (PLATE 1)
Size: 16–22
Thread: black
Tail: grizzly hackle barbules
Body: stripped peacock quill
Head: peacock herl

CRANEFLY LARVA (PLATE 4)
Size: 6–14, 2X to 4X long
Thread: brown
Body: gray yarn
Rib: gold wire
Head: dark brown fur

DOBSONFLY LARVA
(HELLGRAMMITE) (PLATE 4)
Size: 2–10, 6X long
Thread: black
Tail: black hackle barbules
Abdomen/thorax: dark brown coarse fur
Rib: black monocord
Back/wing case: black raffia
Gills: picked-out abdomen fur
Legs: black grizzly hen hackle
Antennae: black goose biots

ALDER FLY LARVA (PLATE 4)
Size: 12–14, 4X long
Thread: olive
Tail: olive marabou fibers
Abdomen: yellow/brown fur
Thorax: light brown fur
Legs: olive hackle

DAMSELFLY NYMPH (PLATE 4)
Size: 6–10, 2X to 3X long
Thread: black
Tail: peacock sword tips
Abdomen/thorax: dark olive fur
Legs: olive grizzly hen hackle
Eyes: melted monofilament

DRAGONFLY NYMPH (PLATE 4)
Size: 4–10, 4X long
Thread: olive
Abdomen/thorax: dark olive dubbing
Back: olive raffia
Rib: copper wire
Legs: olive grizzly hen hackle
Head: dark olive dubbing
Wing case/head: olive raffia
Eyes: melted monofilament

ASSAM DRAGON (PLATE 4)
Size: 4–10, 1X to 3X long
Thread: brown
Body: brown seal-fur strip, wrapped
Legs: brown hen grizzly hackle

RYAN'S SOFT-SHELL CRAYFISH (PLATE 4)
Size: 4–8, 2X long
Thread: brown
Body: tan rabbit fur/Antron dubbing
Carapace: light bucktail, folded from bend
  over body to form thorax shell and tail
Rib: brown monocord
Claws: fox fur fibers tied in midway and
  extending only to bend
Legs: partridge hackle on thorax
Gills: picked-out underfur
*Note: Fly can be tied with hook in standard
position or weighted along top of shank and
tied upside down to keep it weedless.*

SCUD (PLATE 1)
Size: 10–18
Thread: olive
Body: coarse olive dubbing
Overbody: cellophane
Rib: gold wire
Antennae: woodduck barbules
Legs: picked-out underfur
*Note: Tie in a variety of colors from dark olive
to orange to pink.*

SOWBUG (PLATE 1)
Size: 10–18
Thread: brown
Body: coarse brown dubbing, picked out
Overbody: cellophane
Rib: copper wire

BIBLIOGRAPHY

Bates, Joseph D., Jr. *Streamers and Buck-tails: The Big Fish Flies.* New York: Alfred A. Knopf, 1987.

Borger, Gary A. *Nymphing: A Basic Book.* Harrisburg, Pa., Stackpole Books, 1979.

Brooks, Charles E. *Nymph Fishing for Larger Trout.* New York: Lyons & Burford, Publishers, 1976.

Brooks, Charles E. *The Trout and the Stream.* New York: Lyons & Burford, Publishers, 1988.

Caucci, Al, and Bob Nastasi. *Hatches II: A Complete Guide to Fishing the Hatches of North American Trout Streams.* New York: Nick Lyons Books, 1986.

Flick, Art. *Art Flick's New Streamside Guide to Naturals and Their Imitations.* New York: Nick Lyons Books, 1969.

LaFontaine, Gary. *Caddisflies.* New York: Lyons & Burford, Publishers, 1981.

Leisenring, James, and Vernon S. Hidy. *The Art of Tying the Wet Fly and Fishing the Flymph.* New York: Crown Publishers, Inc., 1971.

Leiser, Eric, and Robert H. Boyle. *Stoneflies for the Angler: How to Know Them, Tie Them, and Fish Them.* Harrisburg, Pa.: Stackpole Books, 1982.

Merwin, John. *Streamer-Fly Fishing.* New York: Lyons & Burford, Publishers, 1991.

Nemes, Sylvester. *The Soft-Hackled Fly: A Trout Fisherman's Guide.* Harrisburg, Pa.: Stackpole Books, 1993.

Pobst, Dick. *Trout Stream Insects: An Orvis Streamside Guide.* New York: Lyons & Burford, Publishers, 1990.

Rosborough, E. H. "Polly." *Tying and Fishing the Fuzzy Nymphs.* 4th rev. ed. Harrisburg, Pa.: Stackpole Books, 1988.

Schwiebert, Ernest. *Nymphs.* New York: Winchester Press, 1973.

Solomon, Larry, and Eric Leiser. *The Caddis and the Angler.* Rev. and enl. ed. New York: Lyons & Burford, Publishers, 1990.

Stewart, Dick, and Farrow Allen. *Flies for Trout.* North Conway, N.H.: Mountain Pond Publishing, 1993.

Swisher, Doug, and Carl Richards. *Emergers.* New York: Lyons & Burford, Publishers, 1991.

Whitlock, Dave. *Dave Whitlock's Guide to Aquatic Trout Foods.* New York: Lyons & Burford, Publishers, 1982.

INDEX